Gary Jobson puts his trust in classics.

Perpetual Spirit

Having competed successfully in a variety of boats, Gary Jobson's choice for himself is a classic Herreshoff 28-footer, whose graceful design will never go out of style. The same aesthetic is reflected in his timepiece.

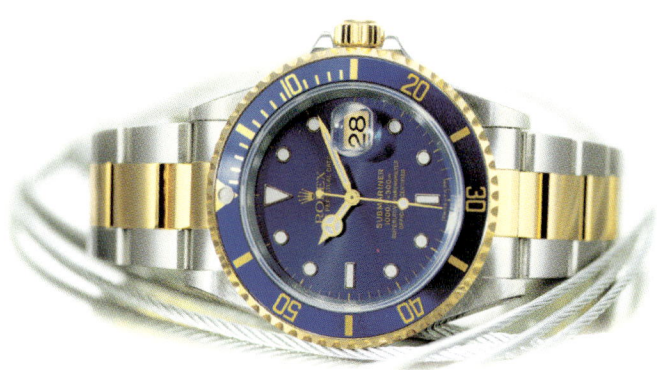

ROLEX

Rolex Oyster Perpetual Submariner in stainless steel and 18kt gold.
Officially Certified Swiss Chronometer.

REEDS
Jewelers

Westfield Shoppingtown Independence   910.799.6810

Rolex, Oyster Perpetual and Submariner are trademarks.

www.wilmingtontoday.com

Welcome TO WILMINGTON and the Cape Fear Coast

Cape Fear Images, Inc.
5621 Athens Lane
Wilmington, NC 28405

(910) 392-5228
(910) 313-2523 fax
(888) 755-0550 toll-free

Publisher & Chief Designer
Kathleen Beall Meyer

Editor & Writer
John H. Meyer

Webmaster
Travis Dent

Production Manager
Natallia Nemes

Sales Representative
Lauren Hahn

Photography by
Dick Parrott
John Meyer

Special thanks to
Cape Fear Coast Convention & Visitors Bureau

Other photos
Airborne Museum
Brunswick Tourism
Battleship North Carolina
Brownie Harris
Cameron Art Museum
Cape Fear Museum
Cape Fear Riverboats
Jay Curley
Richard K. Davis
Duplin Tourism
Mike Hewett
N.C. Marine Fisheries
N.C. Aquarium
Pauline Purdum
Pete Vinal
Southport-Oak Island Chamber
UNCW

Unless credited otherwise, all contents © 2003, Cape Fear Images, Inc.

ISBN 0-9729573-0-8

Contents

About Wilmington	5	Dining	33
Historic downtown	7	Recreation & sports	39
The beaches	8	Golf	41
Parks & natural areas	14	Boating	44
Attractions & museums	15	Fishing	46
Historic sites	18	Hunting	48
Battleship North Carolina	21	Amusements	49
Aquarium	22	Cameron Art Museum	50
Area map	24	Art galleries	51
Traffic	25	Performing arts	54
Tours & cruises	26	Night life	55
Festivals	31	Shopping	57
Weather	31	Day trips	60

Wilmington Today
A Guide to Cape Fear Leisure

Letter from the Editors

We hope you find this guidebook, the 21st annual edition, to be useful to you during your stay on the Cape Fear Coast.

It features several new attractions: The North Carolina Aquarium at Fort Fisher, The Louise Wells Cameron Art Museum, the visitor center at the Fort Fisher historic site and the Cape Fear Serpentarium Downtown.

This book is provided for your convenience by the management of the area's hotels, B&B inns, rental cottages and condos. Please leave it in the room for the next guests.

The book is also on sale at area bookstores. Or we will gladly mail you a copy for $15.95. Send a check and your address to:

Cape Fear Images, Inc.
5621 Athens Lane
Wilmington, NC 28405

For credit card orders, call 392-5228.

Wilmington Today is written, edited and designed by long-time Wilmington residents. This guidebook was founded in 1983 as "A Guide to Cape Fear Leisure" and has been published annually since then.

We welcome your suggestions about additions or improvements to future editions.

For current schedules and updates, our interactive database of visitor services, links to many useful local web sites, and much more, see our web site at WilmingtonToday.com

on the web: www.wilmingtontoday.com   **email:** editor@wilmingtontoday.com

Unique COMMUNITIES

WILMINGTON'S PLACE IN THE WORLD

Wilmington's human landscape bears imprints from all over the world.

By the 1990s, this was one of the nation's fastest-growing metropolitan areas.

Within a 40-mile radius are some of the East Coast's finest beaches.

Each beach town has its own unique flavor and personality

Until the early 20th century, Wilmington was North Carolina's largest city.

Don't call Wilmington a small town. This is a small *city*, thank you, with a long cosmopolitan pedigree. It has always had an urban sophistication and cultural amenities out of proportion to its size.

The center of one of the nation's fastest growing regions in the 1980s and '90s, Wilmington now extends from the Cape Fear River to the Atlantic Intracoastal Waterway. The city's population is 90,000, according to a 2000 state estimate. The urbanized area extends well into New Hanover County. This is North Carolina's second smallest in size, but among its most densely developed, with 163,455 people in 2001.

That growth has spread to the adjoining coastal communities. Just across the Cape Fear from Wilmington is Brunswick County, which stretches to the South Carolina line. Blessed with beautiful beaches, congenial weather for year-round golfing, and proximity to the booming Wilmington and Myrtle Beach markets, Brunswick County's population has more than doubled in the past 25 years.

To the North, Pender County is also experiencing rapid growth. It's not just the beach-and-golf strip that includes Topsail Island and Hampstead. New industry, shopping and neighborhoods are springing up along the I-40 corridor, a quick commute to Wilmington.

HISTORY

What's now Wilmington was first settled in the early 1700s, about the time the last pirates were routed from North Carolina waters. New Hanover County and an Anglican parish were founded here in 1729. By the 1730s, a town was taking shape where the Cape Fear River's two branches meet.

Chartered in 1739, Wilmington quickly outstripped its rivals. For nearly 200 years it was the largest city in North Carolina. A strategic seaport, it played vital roles in the Revolutionary War, Civil War, and World War II.

In the postwar era, more and more visitors discovered the region's charms, and a steady influx of new residents came to stay.

CULTURE

America's oldest community theater group is the Thalian Association, with origins in Revolutionary times. The Thalians perform in Thalian Hall, a showplace theater built as part of City Hall in the 1850s, when it could hold 10 percent of the city's population.

Wilmington also has a newly expanded art museum, the Louise Wells Cameron Museum, which opened its new building in April 2002. Our active local arts community is represented by a diverse range of galleries.

Other major institutions include a public university with a world-class reputation in marine science, rapidly growing community colleges in Wilmington and Brunswick County, and a major regional medical center.

Public radio station WHQR at 91.3 FM brings classical music, opera, news and public affairs programming. It also provides air time for styles including jazz, blues, folk and bluegrass. Other musical assets include an active community orchestra, regular visits by the North Carolina Symphony, and nationally renowned touring performers.

SEE: Museums on page 15.
SEE: Art museums & galleries on page 50.
SEE: Performing arts on page 54.

Our diverse people

Wilmington's human landscape bears imprints from all over the world. Early populations of African, English, Irish, Scots and French Huguenot origin were enriched by Protestant and Jewish immigrants from Germany before the Civil War.

Other important immigrant groups have come from Greece, the Netherlands and Poland. Recently, Wilmington has welcomed newcomers from Asia. An important and growing Latino community, mostly with roots in Mexico and Central America, is adding new styles to our cultural mix.

Starting after the Civil War, and increasingly since World War II, the city's southern flavor has been leavened by "Yankee" newcomers. Servicemen who discovered Wilmington when stationed nearby returned to vacation, and eventually to live, in the postwar decades. Another important wave of migration is the children and grandchildren of North Carolinians, especially African Americans, who went north in search of better lives decades ago. Many of these transplanted Southerners are returning to ancestral communities seeking a less stressful lifestyle, milder climate, and renewed family ties.

Our economy

Through its history, waves of change have passed over Wilmington. Always a seaport, at times it has been a shipbuilding town. Confederate ironclads built here met ignoble fates, but 243 Liberty and Victory ships made here helped turn the tide of victory during World War II. For more than a century, Wilmington was a major railroad center, with as many as seven lines radiating from the city's stations and roundhouses. In the 20th Century, high-tech manufacturing found a home here, with major employers making fiber optics, jet engine parts, and nuclear fuel. New entries include software and pharmaceutical research.

Our most glamorous industry has earned Wilmington the nickname "Hollywood East." Starting with Dino DeLaurentiis' 1983 production of *Firestarter*, the movies have been part of the city's ambience and an important source of jobs.

As farm crops evolved, so did the cargoes that crowded Wilmington's wharves and made its fortunes. Rice in the 18th Century gave way to cotton in the 19th and tobacco and produce in the 20th. As the 21st Century opened, industrial-style pork and poultry farming are supplanting tobacco, and cotton is making a comeback. Pine tar and other "naval stores" yielded to lumber, pulp and paper as the products of the area's forests.

Echoes of bygone crops can be seen in abandoned rice fields, the Cotton Exchange, and decaying curing barns in former tobacco fields.

Tourism

Beautiful beaches have attracted tourists since the late 1800s. Until recently, poor transportation made the region a hidden treasure, known only to an adventurous minority of vacationers. Interstate 40's opening in 1990 made Wilmington and nearby beaches an easy driving destination. This sparked a boom in tourism, and accelerated growth in housing, shopping, dining and entertainment.

Downtown Wilmington, not long ago a run-down district shunned even by locals, is now a tourist attraction.

Shopping

A large indoor mall, opened in 1979 and expanded in 2001, draws shoppers from the entire region. A wide range of other retail centers serve every taste, from discount outlets to upscale boutiques and specialty stores.

SEE: Shopping on page 56.

Recreation

Water, open space and mild climate make the area ideal for recreation. Water sports, fishing and golf are the "Big Three" for residents and visitors alike. Running, cycling, tennis and hunting all enjoy large followings.

Sports fans have baseball and soccer in the summer, and college basketball in the winter.

SEE: Sports on page 39.
SEE: Boating on page 44.
SEE: Fishing on page 46.

MIKE HEWETT
On location downtown

The 'Fear' Factor

Many first-time visitors to our corner of the world are puzzled by the "Cape Fear" name attached to so many places and institutions.

Some associate it with the 1962 movie starring Gregory Peck and Robert Mitchum, or the 1991 Robert DeNiro-Nick Nolte remake. (Neither was filmed in Wilmington.)

North Carolina's southeastern corner is called the "Cape Fear Coast," or "Lower Cape Fear," for the Cape Fear River and its main tributary, the Northeast Cape Fear River. These join at downtown Wilmington, the reason the city is here.

The river got its name from the cape, at the tip of Bald Head Island.

Why "Fear?"

Early maps - from the 1500s and 1600s - use "Cape Fear" or the Latin "Promontorium Tremendum," which means pretty much the same thing. North Carolina's capes are serious hazards to sailors. Treacherous currents and shoals, and sometimes fierce weather (including hurricanes) have wrecked hundreds of ships through the centuries.

Don't be scared!

The name is sometimes attributed to Giovanni da Verrazzano, the Italian explorer, who came ashore near Cape Fear in 1524. It most likely was assigned later, originally to Cape Lookout, 100 miles up the coast. The earliest English explorer, one William Hilton, mis-read his map and ended up here. His mistake, in 1662, permanently assigned the "Fear" to our cape, and region.

However it's used, don't let the name bother you. We're used to it around here. But for our guests who aren't, let us take the "fear" out of your Cape Fear vacation.

Downtown
and the Riverfront

DICK PARROTT

JOHN MEYER
The Riverwalk is a promenade along the Cape Fear River. The newest stretch runs from near Dock to Nun streets.

We love Downtown Wilmington. It has always been our region's heart and soul. The Cape Fear River, block after block of carefully restored 18th-, 19th- and early-20th-century buildings, fascinating shops, fine dining, lively night life: all contribute to Downtown's unique charm.

But it wasn't always like this.

A major revitalization effort, with public and private investments, reversed a trend of blight and decay starting in the 1970s.

Today, Downtown is a bustling destination, its streets crowded with pedestrians day and night. Many of them are visitors, conventioneers staying at one of Downtown's hotel, or tourists from one of the beaches checking out our "other" waterfront resort.

ANCHORS

For a first visit to Downtown, consider starting at one of the complexes of shops and restaurants in restored historic buildings. The buildings and courtyards of The Cotton Exchange, on North Front Street, once housed the city's cotton traders. Chandler's Wharf, at Water and Ann streets, offers fine shopping and dining with romantic river views. Both offer free customer parking.

Between these "anchors" are many other shops, eateries and attractions.

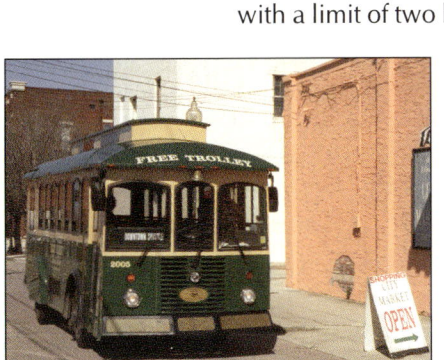

JOHN MEYER
Free trolley bus runs a shuttle loop.

JOHN MEYER
Parking is free the first hour, after 5 p.m. and on weekends in new deck next to library on North Third Street.

STREETS

Downtown's backbone is Market Street. Some of the city's oldest buildings, and newest businesses, line this charming tree-shaded boulevard.

Water Street is lined with riverside shops, hotels, restaurants and condominiums. Riverfront Park and Riverwalk, a public promenade, give pedestrians great views.

Front Street has a wide range of retail shops, restaurants and office buildings. The City Stage Theatre is in the old Masonic Temple building on North Front Street.

On Second and Third streets are public buildings, including the library, City Hall, Courthouse, and some of the city's finest old churches. Part of City Hall is Thalian Hall, the showplace antebellum theater.

For downtown locations, SEE map on page 57.

PARKING

Parking is available in public decks and lots, some private lots serving individual shops and restaurants, and metered on-street spaces. Meter rates are 50 cents an hour, with a limit of two hours most places but one hour on North Front Street. On-street parking is free after 6:30 p.m. Public lots and decks offer all-day parking for $5. Rates are $1 an hour, free after 5 p.m. and on weekends, with these exceptions:

The deck next to the library between Second and Third streets is free for the first hour and free for library patrons.

The lot at Second and Market streets offers unlimited evening parking is $3.

The private deck between Front and Water streets offers all-day parking for $3.25, free evenings and weekends.

Another deck is under construction at Second, Market and Princess streets.

GETTING AROUND

Free shuttle: The Wilmington Transit Authority operates a free trolley on a continuous loop up Front Street and down Water and Second streets.

River taxi: Regular shuttle service carries passengers between Downtown and the Battleship North Carolina.

SEE: Tours on page 26.

www.wilmingtontoday.com

TIPS FOR BEACHGOERS

Use sunscreen. Always. Because water and beach sand reflect ultraviolet rays, you'll burn faster at the beach than inland. Sunscreens protect best if applied before you get into the sun. Use a Sun Protection Factor (SPF) of at least 8; young children should have a 30 SPF. If a good tan is your goal, sunscreen will help you avoid burning and peeling. If you are pale to begin with, use a higher SPF on your first few days in the sun; you can shift to a lower factor toward the end of your stay.

Hats, shirts, sunglasses and umbrellas let you enjoy your time on the beach longer without subjecting your skin or eyes to harmful rays.

Protect dunes. When crossing dunes, stay on paths or walkways. Walking on dunes harms a fragile ecosystem that helps protect property from hurricanes.

Don't litter. Buried trash, including cigarette butts, quickly surfaces again. Use trash cans if available; bring a trash bag and carry your trash out if necessary.

Alcoholic beverages are prohibited on all public beaches within town limits and at other lifeguard-protected public beaches. Glass containers are banned in many places and a bad idea everywhere.

Pets are prohibited on the beach in many towns. Where leashed dogs are permitted, be courteous and clean up your pet's waste. It is a serious health hazard, not to mention disgusting.

Pier perils: Swimmers and surfers should stay well clear of fishing piers. Bare skin is no match for dangling fishhooks and barnacle-covered pilings.

Surfing may be restricted to limited areas or prescribed hours on some beaches. Check with lifeguards if in doubt. In all cases, be courteous. Don't crowd your fellow surfers, and stay away from areas with large numbers of swimmers.

Obey lifeguards. At many beaches, flags on lifeguard stands warn of dangerous surf. Red flags mean powerful rip currents can endanger even experienced swimmers; stay out of the water.

CAPE FEAR COAST CONVENTION & VISITORS BUREAU

Beaches
Sea, sand and sky

Within a 40-mile radius of Wilmington lie some of the East Coast's finest beaches.

That definition doesn't apply if your idea of a fine beach includes neon, high-rises and gaudy attractions. More than a dozen distinct oceanfront communities lie between Camp Lejeune and the South Carolina line. Each has its own flavor and personality. None aspires to the sort of high-octane character found at better-known resorts in other states. (But if that appeals to you, consider a fun day-trip to the bright lights of Myrtle Beach, just an hour's drive away.)

We even have significant stretches of that great rarity: Totally wild beach.

Of the seaside resorts, the closest to Wilmington is Wrightsville Beach. Separated from the city by the Intracoastal Waterway, Wrightsville Beach has carefully guarded its single-family atmosphere. Favored by day-trippers, it offers rental cottages and resort hotels for vacationers.

Just a few miles south is Pleasure Island, which includes Carolina Beach, Kure Beach and Fort Fisher.

Up the coast is Topsail Island and the towns of Topsail Beach, Surf City and North Topsail Beach.

CONVENTION & VISITORS BUREAU
Two barrier islands: Wrightsville Beach and Masonboro Island

Across the Cape Fear River, Brunswick County boasts a striking assortment of beach towns: Caswell Beach, Oak Island, Holden Beach, Ocean Isle Beach and Sunset Beach, plus the riverside town of Southport. Then there is Bald Head Island, the state's southernmost point, a subtropical setting accessible only by boat.

BARRIER ISLANDS

Except for parts of Pleasure Island, all the area's beaches are barrier islands. These long, narrow geological structures were formed – and are still shaped -- by wind, waves, tides and currents. They protect the mainland from the sea, and shelter the fertile marshes and sounds that nurture our seafood resources. The Intracoastal Waterway passes between beaches and mainland.

This physical separation, spanned by high-rise bridges and drawbridges, makes each island a distinctive place unto itself. Crossing the bridge marks "the beach" as a special place apart.

WRIGHTSVILLE BEACH

Oldest of the area's beach towns, Wrightsville Beach started as a resort in the late 19th Century. It was incorporated in 1899 and has always been closely linked to Wilmington.

www.wilmingtontoday.com

The town's 20th Century history is punctuated by fires and hurricanes, but it has always bounced back. Today, it is a mix of permanent homes, rental cottages, condos and multi-story hotels. Several business districts cater to locals and visitors. Excellent restaurants offer fresh local seafood, often with spectacular waterfront views.

To fight the erosion that is a fact of barrier island life, Wrightsville Beach has a regular program of beach renourishment, using sand dredged from nearby Masonboro Inlet to build up the shore and dunes. Critics complain about the cost, split between federal dollars and local hotel taxes, but the rebuilt beach and dune proved its value during the hurricanes of the 1990s. Sheltered by the sandy expanse, Wrightsville suffered relatively little damage from storm waves.

Town amenities include an extensive park, a wetland preserve, and a state-operated boat ramp. Runners and other fitness buffs throng "The Loop," a two-and-a-half-mile circuit of paved walks and bridges around the town's two islands. The town's history is preserved in the Wrightsville Beach Museum, a restored beach cottage in the park. SEE: Museums on page 16.

To get there: U.S. 74 (Market Street and Eastwood Road) or U.S. 76 (Oleander Drive and Wrightsville Avenue) to the drawbridge. The bridge opens to non-commercial boat traffic once an hour, on the hour.

CAROLINA BEACH

Separated from the mainland by Snows Cut, a stretch of the Intracoastal Waterway, Carolina Beach is a popular resort with roots in the 19th Century. Because roads were bad, most early visitors took the steamer *Wilmington* down the Cape Fear River, and rode from a riverside wharf to the seaside by train. The track ran down what's now Harper Avenue.

Joseph Winner originally called his town St. Joseph's. The Winner name didn't stick, but the family did. Joseph's descendants are well-known charter boat skippers.

By the 1940s, paved roads had replaced the riverboat-and-train connection, and amusement places had grown up on the Boardwalk. A new hotel, opening in 2003, is part of the town's campaign to revitalize the Boardwalk area.

A public marina in the center of town is home to the region's largest fleet of charter fishing boats, head

CAPE FEAR COAST CONVENTION & VISITORS BUREAU
A summer sunrise silhouettes strollers over Wrightsville Beach

PETE VINAL
Wrightsville Beach drawbridge opens on the hour for pleasure boats.

BEACH PARKING

Parking is scarce at the beaches, especially the ones closest to Wilmington. Expect to pay, either by meter or pay stations in public parking lots. Be prepared with a supply of quarters and dollar bills; you may not find change on the beach.

Wrightsville Beach: On-street parking is regulated by meters from March 1 through Oct. 31. Parking is free November through February. The meter rate is $1.25 an hour. Meters take quarters only. Public lots with pay stations are found along North Lumina Avenue in the Shell Island section, on South Lumina Avenue near the Oceanic Pier, and at Masonboro Inlet on the far south end. The fine for overtime parking is $15; parking fines must be paid within 72 hours at the Central Parking Systems office at Causeway Drive (U.S. 76) and Live Oak Drive. Restaurant, motel and store lots are strictly limited to patrons; towing is enforced. Blocking driveways will also get a car promptly towed.

Long-term storage of boat trailers is prohibited at the state launching ramp. Spaces there are reserved for boaters while on the water.

Carolina Beach: Parking spaces on main streets are metered from April 1 through Sept. 30. Parking is $1 an hour; a quarter buys 15 minutes. Some public lots are metered; time limits apply to all public spaces year-round. Pay stations in public lots allow all-day parking for $5.

www.wilmingtontoday.com

Carolina Beach's boat basin is home port to the region's leading fleet of recreational fishing boats, which carry anglers offshore or to the Gulf Stream.

PETE VINAL

boats and excursion boats. A state launching ramp provides boat access to the Intracoastal Waterway and nearby Carolina Beach Inlet.

A regular beach renourishment program helps keep the strand wide and easily accessible. At the town's far north end, next to a new fishing pier, a ramp gives fishermen in four-wheel-drive vehicles access to the beach as far as the inlet.

Carolina Beach State Park, along the Cape Fear River and Snows Cut, offers natural areas, a boat ramp and the area's only public campsite.

The original downtown business area, shopping centers, a movie theater and an amusement park are close to the beach.

Visitor accommodations include cottages and condominiums for rent by the week, and numerous "mom-and-pop" motels. The town's first national hotel is expected to open this year.

To get there: N.C. 132 (South College Road) or U.S. 421 (South Third Street and Carolina Beach Road) south to Monkey Junction; then U.S. 421 to Snows Cut Bridge. The bridge gives visitors spectacular first views of the Atlantic and the Cape Fear River.

SEE: Tours on page 26.

KURE BEACH

Tucked snugly against Carolina Beach is Kure Beach, a smaller resort that grew up in parallel starting in the 1870s. Named for Danish-born developer Hans Andersen Kure, it originally was accessible by river steamer and a short train ride. Say the name "cure-E."

Present-day Kure Beach has a few small motels but mostly consists of rental cottages and year-round homes.

A small business district includes restaurants and a fishing pier. It is close to all the attractions of Fort Fisher.

On the town's river side are miles of undeveloped land along Dow Road. This is the safety zone around the Army's Sunny Point ammunition terminal across the river. Another curiosity, straddling U.S. 421 just north of town, is acres of air conditioners, light fixtures, and other metal parts. These are exposed to salt air and harsh sunlight by the LaQue Center for Corrosion Research, based at Wrightsville Beach.

To get there: From Carolina Beach; either follow U.S. 421 (Fort Fisher Boulevard) or take Dow Road (first right off 421 past Snows Cut Bridge.) This avoids Carolina Beach traffic and comes into Kure Beach at K Street.

PETE VINAL
Civil War re-enactor at Fort Fisher Historic Site

FORT FISHER

This unincorporated area gets its name from the massive Civil War fort that was called "The Gibraltar of the Confederacy." Remaining portions are preserved in a State Historic Site, which includes an interpretive visitor center with brand-new exhibits.

Modern Fort Fisher traces its origins to World War II, when the Army used the former Confederate stronghold as an artillery training center, and beach cottages began to spread south from Kure Beach. A former Air Force radar station remains open as a recreation center for military personnel.

Among Fort Fisher's attractions is one of the three North Carolina Aquariums, which features large exhibits on the region's marine life. Also here are a lifeguard-protected public beach, a beach access ramp for four-wheel-drive vehicles, and the terminal of the ferry to Southport.

At the end of U.S. 421 is "The Rocks," a tidal dam built in the 1880s to close New Inlet and stop shoaling in the Cape Fear River channel. A popular hiking and fishing spot, it gives access to the Zeke's Island nature preserve. Use caution: the dam can be slippery, and is dangerous at times of high tide or strong winds.

To get there: U.S. 421 (Fort Fisher Boulevard) south from Kure Beach or Cape Fear River ferry from Southport.

SEE: Historic sites on page 18.
SEE: N.C. Aquarium on page 22.
SEE: Ferry on page 24.

BEACH CHECKLIST:
♦ Tote bag
♦ Sunscreen
♦ Insect repellent
♦ Towels
♦ Flip-flops, sandals or slip-on shoes (sand can get painfully hot)
♦ Sunglasses (polarized is best for glare off water)
♦ Hat, ideally wide-brimmed
♦ Beach chair
♦ Beach umbrella (a sand anchor is handy on breezy days)
♦ Snacks
♦ Drinks (no alcohol or glass bottles)
♦ Camera and film or digital media
♦ Small trash bag (that plastic sack from the variety store will do just fine.)

FIGURE EIGHT ISLAND

Just north of Wrightsville Beach, this private island is open only to property owners and their guests. A guard on the swing drawbridge controls access to the island's roads.

Extensive tidal flats at the ends of the island attract boaters, who anchor by the dozens to enjoy the sand and water during the summer months.

TOPSAIL ISLAND

About half an hour's drive northeast of Wilmington, this 27-mile-long island includes three towns. It extends from New Topsail Inlet to New River Inlet, the boundary of Camp Lejeune.

The island got its name in the 1700s, when only the topsails could be seen on ships sheltered in the deep channel behind the dunes. By the way: it's pronounced "TOP-sul." (It's fun, but not necessary, to add "Arrrr.")

The island was undeveloped until after World War II. During the war, it was a training and recreation area for nearby Camp Davis, an Army anti-aircraft artillery base. After the war, the Navy's fledgling missile program, Operation Bumblebee, conducted tests here. The Navy built a string of concrete observation towers along the island. Most still stand, some now part of newer buildings. Missiles were put together in the Assembly Building in Topsail Beach, which now houses the Missiles and More Museum.

The island's south end is Topsail Beach. It has a fishing pier, bike path and a small business district with restaurants and snack bars.

In the island's center, right across the N.C. 50-210 swing bridge, is Surf City. It has a wide range of housing and the island's largest commercial district, with restaurants, supermarket, nightclubs and fishing pier.

North of Surf City is North Topsail Beach, the island's newest town. It is the site of public beach and boating access points, and a popular fishing area at New River Inlet..

A second bridge from the mainland carries N.C. 210, connecting North Topsail Beach with Sneads Ferry, Camp Lejeune and Jacksonville.

To get there: U.S. 17 north through Hampstead. Right (east) on N.C. 210, which merges with N.C. 50. Follow 50-210 to the bridge. (It opens on the hour.) N.C. 50 to Topsail Beach; N.C. 210 to North Topsail Beach.

From Interstate 40: Exit 408, N.C. 210 east through Hampstead to island. Or exit 398, N.C. 53 east to N.C. 50 south through Holly Ridge to island.

JOHN MEYER
Missile tracking towers from the 1940s have been incorporated into several homes on Topsail Island.

SOUTHPORT

It isn't a beach community, but Southport is a waterfront town of considerable history and charm. A half-hour drive from Wilmington, or a short ferry ride from Fort Fisher, it is the gateway to two true beach resorts: Oak Island and Bald Head Island.

Near the Cape Fear River's mouth, Southport was established in the 1700s as Smithville. Then, as now, it was the base for river pilots who steer ocean-going ships up the river channel to Wilmington. An old pilots' lookout tower still stands in Southport.

It was also the site of Fort Johnston, originally a Royal garrison, and later a U.S. Army post. All that remains is a brick house on the waterfront. Still Army property, it houses the commander of the Sunny Point ordnance terminal just upriver.

Southport has the look of a county seat, which it was until the 1970s when Brunswick County government moved to a central site inland.

A picturesque shopping district, immaculately restored old houses, and broad streets lined with moss-draped live oaks make Southport a visitor's delight. It's also a favorite shooting location for movie companies.

The town's merchants include art, craft and antique dealers; restaurants include traditional seafood houses and a variety of international cuisines.

Other attractions include a large marina and the historic Old Southport Burying Ground. A waterfront park offers good views of North Carolina's oldest and newest lighthouses on Bald Head Island and Oak Island, and of historic Fort Caswell. A visitor with good timing may see a laden container ship inbound from the Far East.

The Bald Head Island ferry terminal is at the end of West Ninth Street, off Howe Street, in Southport. (Wiseacres will also appreciate the names of three of Southport's oldest streets: Lord, Howe, Dry.)

Just out of town are the western terminal of the state ferry to Fort Fisher, and the Brunswick Nuclear Plant. On the road from Wilmington are Colo-

JOHN MEYER
Officers' quarters from Fort Johnston still stand on Southport's waterfront.

BRUNSWICK COUNTY TOURISM
Beautifully preserved houses lend Victorian charm to Southport.

www.wilmingtontoday.com

Bald Head Island combines a luxury resort with vast nature preserves.
BRUNSWICK COUNTY TOURISM

nial and Civil War sites at Brunswick Town, and Orton Plantation Gardens.

To get there: U.S. 17-74-76 west across Cape Fear Memorial Bridge. At N.C. 133 exit, left (south) toward Southport. 133 joins N.C. 87. At Southport, 87 intersects N.C. 211. Left (east) on 211 to downtown Southport.

Alternate route: U.S. 421 south to Fort Fisher. Ferry to Southport. N.C. 211 into downtown Southport.

SEE: Historic sites on page 18.
SEE: Ferry on page 24.
SEE: Festivals on page 31.

BALD HEAD ISLAND

Unique nature preserve, luxury resort, quaint village, golfer's paradise: Bald Head is all of these. At the mouth of the Cape Fear River, the island includes Cape Fear itself. This point of sand marks where the coastline swings from a north-south line to run east-west. The island's name comes from a bare sand dune that looked like a bald head poking through the woods.

At the entrance to Wilmington's harbor, and near dangerous shoals, Bald Head was the site of one of the United States' first lighthouses. The first tower, built in 1794, was lost to erosion. Its replacement, built in 1817, still stands: North Carolina's oldest lighthouse. Called "Old Baldy," the tower has been carefully restored for visitors. It no longer serves as a navigation beacon. It was replaced in 1903 by a taller steel tower, now long gone. The present Oak Island Lighthouse went up across the river in 1958.

The restored keeper's cottage is now a museum.

Modern-day Bald Head Island is a village with a cadre of year-round residents; a retreat from modern pressures with no automobiles; an upscale vacation resort featuring fine beaches and golf courses; and a vast preserve, which sets aside from development a majority of the island and surrounding wetlands. The village has a small grocery store, a gift shop, and two waterfront restaurants.

Oak Island Light as seen from Caswell Beach shoreline
BRUNSWICK COUNTY TOURISM

Close to the warm Gulf Stream, Bald Head enjoys North Carolina's only subtropical climate, with palms and other species that thrive nowhere else in the state.

Access is only by private ferry. Round-trip toll is $15 for passengers. Residents and visitors get around with golf carts, bicycles or on foot.

To get there: Advance ferry reservations are required. For schedules, call 457-5003. Ferry dock is on West Ninth Street, off N.C. 211.

SEE: Golf on page 41.

BEACH SAFETY:

Beach and ocean are fun, but also subject to great natural forces. Basic precautions can help keep you safe.

Rip currents: The backwash from waves can carry a swimmer away from shore, but the currents are narrow. To escape, swim parallel to the beach. Fighting a rip current will quickly exhaust you. Warning signs on the beaches tell you how to spot a rip current, and what to do if you get into one. A red flag on a lifeguard stand means heavy surf and dangerous rip currents: Stay out of the water.

Tides: The sea's twice-daily rise and fall can imperil the unwary. If exploring exposed sand flats at low tide, pay attention to which way the tide is moving. Don't let rising water or swift outflows take you by surprise.

Inlet currents: Strong tidal flows can quickly sweep an unwary swimmer or wader into deep water. Inlets can also have unpredictable effects in the nearby surf zone. Broad sand flats are inviting places to wade, explore and play, but treacherous at high tide. The best advice about swimming near inlets is simple: Don't.

Sunburn: Ultraviolet rays can quickly damage unprotected skin. Even a few hours of exposure can cause a vacation-spoiling sunburn. Use sunscreen, make sure your children do too, and replenish it if you're in the water a lot or sweating. Don't forget ears and the tops of feet. Whether visiting Bald Head Island or not, protect your noggin if you don't have a full head of hair.

Northern visitors should know that a few hundred miles of latitude, and the reflective power of sand and seawater, greatly magnify the sun's power on a North Carolina beach. If you do overdo it, stay out of the sun for a day or two. There is plenty to see and do away from the beach. When you do get back into the sun, use the strongest sunscreen available.

Heat: It's easy to get dehydrated when temperatures are in the 80s or 90s. Especially if exercising, drink plenty of water or sports drinks. High humidity can limit your body's ability to cool itself by sweating. Consider rescheduling that tennis game or five-mile run for early morning or evening, when temperatures and humidity are more moderate.

Insect bites: Every Southern coastal community has jokes about its "state bird." Our sizable local 'skeeters can be a nuisance on overcast days or still evenings. A supply of insect repellent is never a bad idea at the beach or near water or woods. Most brands also repel biting flies that can turn up in late summer.

Oak Island

The island comprises two towns, the larger of which is also called Oak Island. This town was formed in 1999 by merging the former Long Beach and Yaupon Beach.

A single high-rise bridge crosses to the former Yaupon Beach section. This main commercial district includes a fishing pier. The former Long Beach, true to its name, stretches eight miles west to Lockwood Folly Inlet. Oak Island has many rental opportunities for vacationers. Just across the bridge is Brunswick County Airport, which serves small private aircraft.

To get there: From Southport, N.C. 211 west. 211 merges with N.C. 133. Left (south) on 133 to bridge.

Caswell Beach

This tiny town gets its name from Fort Caswell at Oak Island's eastern tip. It's owned by the North Carolina Baptist Assembly, which uses it for church meetings and retreats. Caswell Beach has no commercial district.

It's home to the Coast Guard's Oak Island station. Standing 169 feet above the station is Oak Island Lighthouse, North Carolina's newest and the nation's brightest. The tower was built in 1958; its black, gray and white identifying bands were cast into the concrete structure rather than painted.

To get there: From Oak Island bridge, follow Caswell Beach Road.

Holden Beach

This town of single-family homes and cottages was developed, starting in the 1950s, by the Holden family, which bought the island in 1756. A non-commercial resort, Holden Beach is perfect for vacationers looking for peace and quiet, an uncrowded beach, and outstanding fishing and seafood. Within minutes of the high-rise bridge are many excellent golf courses.

To get there: U.S. 17 to Shallotte, N.C. 130 south to the bridge.

Ocean Isle Beach

Like its neighbors, Ocean Isle Beach was deserted until after World War II when the Williamson family began developing it as a resort. Mostly single-family homes, Ocean Isle has a large condo complex at its west end, and several motels and restaurants.

Ocean Isle is near the heart of the South Brunswick County golf country.

A private general-aviation airstrip is on the mainland nearby.

To get there: U.S. 17 Business to N.C. 179 to N.C. 904.

JOHN MEYER
Love it or hate it: Sunset Beach's one-lane pontoon bridge.

Sunset Beach

In the opinion of many residents, this is one of the last old-fashioned beach resorts, relatively untouched by recent building booms.

Some credit that to the old-fashioned access. The only road to Sunset Beach crosses an antique one-lane pontoon drawbridge. The bridge is one of the town's attractions, featured on many a picture postcard. It's also the chief source of controversy. One camp favors keeping it to moderate development. Others consider it a hazard and want it replaced.

To get there: U.S. 17 south to N.C. 904; south to N.C. 179.

JOHN MEYER
Fishing boats on Calabash Creek.

Calabash

Not a beach town, this waterfront fishing town deserves mention for its world-famous seafood. The signature local cooking style, lightly battered and deep-fried, is now advertised at restaurants hundreds of miles away.

To get there: N.C. 179 west from Sunset Beach, or U.S. 17 south to Calabash Road.

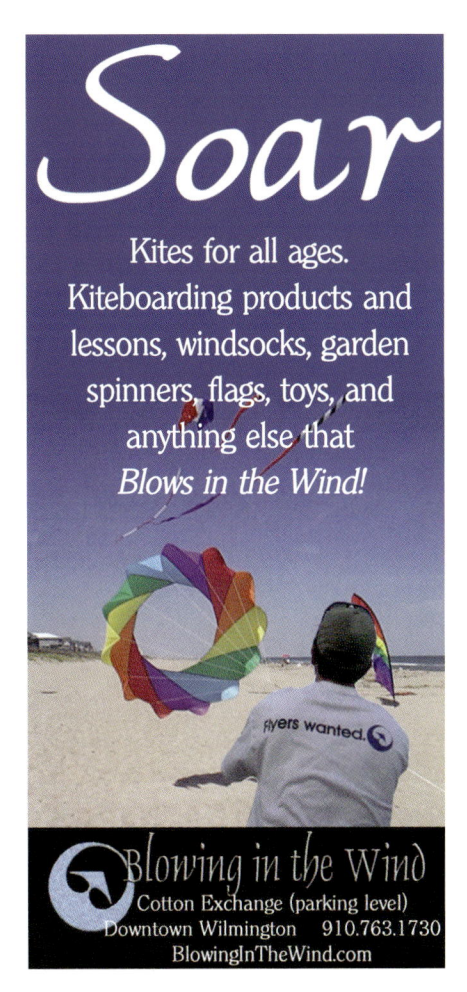

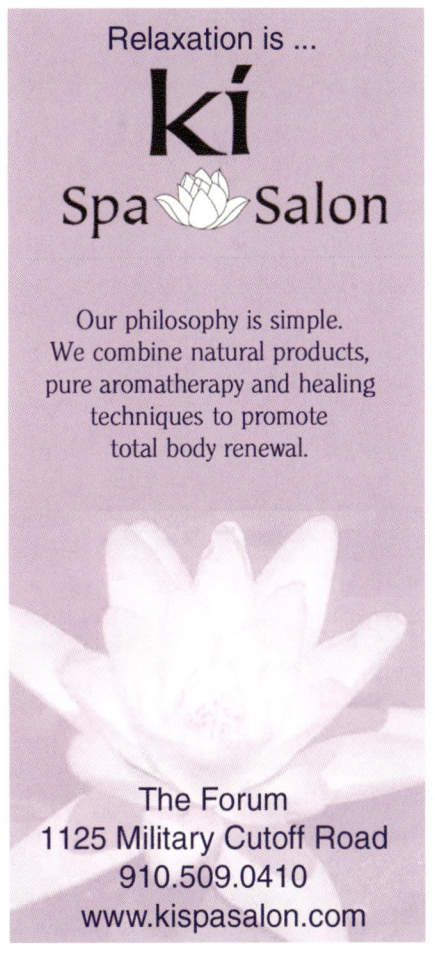

Soar

Kites for all ages. Kiteboarding products and lessons, windsocks, garden spinners, flags, toys, and anything else that *Blows in the Wind!*

Blowing in the Wind
Cotton Exchange (parking level)
Downtown Wilmington 910.763.1730
BlowingInTheWind.com

Relaxation is ...

kí
Spa ❀ Salon

Our philosophy is simple. We combine natural products, pure aromatherapy and healing techniques to promote total body renewal.

The Forum
1125 Military Cutoff Road
910.509.0410
www.kispasalon.com

---

www.wilmingtontoday.com

Nature
Habitats, parks and preserves

Among our region's greatest attractions are its rare and beautiful natural areas. Because intensive development came late to the Cape Fear coast, much of the wild environment survived relatively untouched until a time that could be properly appreciated – and protected.

A visitor is likely to encounter several of these natural habitats:

Barrier island beaches. Narrow sand strips, formed by wind and waves and anchored by dunes, they are nesting grounds for birds and sea turtles.

Maritime forest. In sight of the ocean, a dense canopy of foliage is caused by salt spray killing the most exposed branches of hardy trees.

Salt marsh. These wetlands are among the richest habitats on the planet. They are nurseries for many of the most valuable seafood species.

River estuary. Here the tides produce a rich mix of fresh and salt water. Many fish species mingle and breed here, as do large sea birds.

Blackwater swamp. The Cape Fear and its tributaries are lined by forested wetlands. Tannins released by decaying vegetation tint these waters, home to freshwater game fish, otter and bear.

Pine savanna and Carolina bay. Shaded by longleaf pines and cleared by wildfire, the savannas are home to many rare plants, including insect-eating venus' flytraps. Carolina bays are mysterious oval wetlands.

For more on the region's natural heritage, see **wilmingtontoday.com**

SEE: Tours & cruises on page 26.
SEE: Boating on page 44.
SEE: Fishing on page 46.

THE WILD BEACHES

For those who don't mind roughing it, the Cape Fear Coast offers several rare undeveloped beaches accessible to hikers, four-wheel-drive vehicles or by boat.

Carolina Beach north end: Four-wheel-drives can get to a mile of open beach. Travel lanes are marked with stakes. Dunes are private property; trespassing is prohibited.

Fort Fisher: The 4WD ramp is off Loggerhead Road, which leads to the new N.C. Aquarium. Access may be restricted during sea turtle nesting times. Nesting areas for certain endangered sea-bird species may also be posted.

JOHN MEYER
Maritime forest at Fort Fisher.

Masonboro Island: This eight-mile-long barrier island is the longest undeveloped beach south of Cape Lookout National Seashore. Mostly state-owned, Masonboro is an estuarine preserve. Reach the north end by boat from Wrightsville Beach, or the south end from Carolina Beach.

Bird Island: This mile-long island is tucked against the South Carolina line. A state sanctuary, it's accessible on foot from Sunset Beach.

A unique amenity is a mailbox, labeled "Kindred Spirit." Inside are pens and a notebook, which for two decades have become a collective journal of the island's visitors.

Thousands have written about the island, nature, solitude, life itself.

CAROLINA BEACH STATE PARK

On the banks of the Cape Fear River and Snows Cut, this park includes rare habitats for carnivorous plants, including venus' flytrap, pitcher plants, butterwort and bladderwort. Exhibits at the park visitor center focus on these insect-eating oddities, and the importance of fire to this ecosystem, a mix of woods, marshes and ponds set amid ancient sand dunes.

Amenities include camping, hiking trails, and a marina and boat ramp, all within minutes of the oceanfront. Admission for day use, including picnicking and hiking, is free.

The campground, under pine and oak trees near Snows Cut, has 83 spaces with picnic tables and grill. Drinking water, restrooms and hot showers are nearby. No RV hookups. Sites are rented on first come, first serve basis; nightly fee is $12; campers over 62 pay $10. Two group campsites are available by prior reservation.

Two launching ramps and 40 boat slips are available at the marina, which offers quick access to the Cape Fear, and through Snows Cut to the Intracoastal Waterway and the Atlantic Ocean. The marina sells fuel and snacks. The ramp fee is $4.

Park gates open at 8 a.m. daily, and close after dark: 6 p.m. November through February; 7 p.m. March and October; 8 p.m. April and September; and 10 p.m. May through August. The park office closes at 5 p.m. daily. Office 458-8206; marina 458-7770.

To get there: From Wilmington, take U.S. 421 south to Snows Cut Bridge. Immediately after crossing bridge, take first right to Dow Road. State Park Road is second right.

LAKE WACCAMAW STATE PARK

This park offers access to the cool, tea-colored waters of this unique lake and adjoining wetland forest.

Largest of the enigmatic Carolina Bays, Lake Waccamaw is home to several very rare fish and mollusk species found nowhere else on earth.

The park offers access to the southern edge of the lake's 14-mile shoreline. Hiking trails and boardwalks pass through the forest and into the lake. A tree-shaded picnic area has access to restrooms and drinking water.

A public boat ramp is just outside the park gates. A primitive campsite is available first-come, first served.

Park gates open at 8 a.m. daily, and close at dusk. The park office closes at 5 p.m. daily. (910) 646-4748.

To get there: U.S. 74-76 west. Follow signs to the lake and the park.

Attractions
MUSEUMS & MORE

Museums large and small interpret the unique history and culture of our region.

Battlefields from Revolution and Civil War preserve sites that helped form a nation.

Carefully restored houses are showcases of life from the 18th and 19th centuries.

Wilmington isn't big on bright lights and splashy shows. But there are lots of places to have fun.

BROWNIE HARRIS for CAMERON ART MUSEUM

Cape Fear Museum

The area's largest museum and the state's oldest, the Cape Fear Museum has exhibits that reflect the region's social and natural history. "Waves and Currents: The Lower Cape Fear Story," is a 6,000-square-foot exhibit that visually traces scenes from early settlers, the bustling commerce of the Cape Fear River, the battle for Fort Fisher and other historical events. The Michael Jordan Discovery Gallery explores the natural history of the Cape Fear and has artifacts from hometown hero Michael Jordan's youth.

The museum puts on several special exhibits a year, including touring shows.

9 a.m.-5 p.m. Monday-Saturday, 2-5 p.m. Sunday, closed on Mondays between Labor Day and Memorial Day. Admission $5, seniors $4, children 3-17 $1.

814 Market Street. 341-4350.

CAPE FEAR MUSEUM
Cape Fear Museum features this diorama of Wilmington's Civil War-era waterfront.

Wilmington Railroad Museum

Wilmington was once a leading railroad town. The Atlantic Coast Line had its headquarters here until 1960. The railroad museum's exhibits span the time of the Wilmington and Weldon -- world's longest railroad when new in the 1840s -- into the present. Outdoor exhibits include a newly restored ACL steam locomotive, a caboose and other equipment.

Summer hours (March 15-Oct. 14): 10 a.m.-5 p.m. Monday-Saturday, 1-5 p.m. Sunday. Winter hours (Oct. 15-March 14): 10 a.m.-4 p.m. Monday-Saturday. Adults $3, seniors and military $2, children 3-12 $1.50.

Water Street at Red Cross. 763-2634.

CAPE FEAR COAST CONVENTION & VISITORS BUREAU
Climb aboard a 1900 steam locomotive at Wilmington Railroad Museum.

www.wilmingtontoday.com

Finely detailed model shows major Wrightsville Beach buildings circa 1905, including Lumina, the famous dance pavilion, and a working beach trolley.

WRIGHTSVILLE BEACH MUSEUM OF HISTORY

Housed in one of Wrightsville Beach's oldest buildings, the Myers Cottage, this museum traces the history of the beach from its earliest days, when it was known as "The Hammocks." Restored to early 20th-Century form, the cottage holds a scale model of the town circa 1905, complete with a working "beach car," the electric trolley that ran until the 1930s.

Hours: Noon-6 p.m. Tues-Sun. $3. North Channel Drive. 256-2569.

N.C. MARITIME MUSEUM AT SOUTHPORT

At the mouth of the Cape Fear River, Southport's history has been closely tied to the river and the sea for more than two centuries. The museum, a branch of the N.C. Maritime Museum of Beaufort, showcases that history, starting from the native tribes, through the river pilots who still guide freighters to Wilmington's port, to the modern-day fishing industry.

Exhibits include local pirates and Civil War artifacts.

Hours: 9 a.m. to 5 p.m. Tues- Sat. $2 adults 16-61, $1 seniors. 116 N. Howe Street, Southport. 457-0003.

CP&L VISITORS CENTER

Carolina Power & Light operates this center at its Brunswick Nuclear Plant near Southport. Its exhibits deal with electricity, nuclear power and energy conservation, including short videos on generating electricity.

A pedal-driven generator lets visitors feel how much energy it takes to power a light bulb, TV and other appliances.

Hours: 9 a.m.-4 p.m. Tues-Thurs. Free. N.C. 133 at N.C. 87. 457-6041.

TOPSAIL ISLAND MUSEUM "MISSILES & MORE"

This small museum is in the Topsail Beach Assembly Building, where test missiles were once assembled, now a community meeting place. The museum displays artifacts, including rare color movies, of Operation Bumblebee, the post-World War II Navy missile tests on Topsail Island. It also has photos and memorabilia from Camp Davis, the wartime Army training base at nearby Holly Ridge, and artifacts from area Indians and early settlers.

Hours: 2-4 p.m. daily except Sunday and Wednesday, April 1 through mid-October. Free, donations appreciated. 720 Channel Blvd. (off N.C. 50), Topsail Beach.

Examples of missiles that were tested on Topsail Island in the late 1940s are displayed at Missiles & More Museum.

N.C. MILITARY HISTORY MUSEUM

This small museum is on the grounds of the Fort Fisher Air Force Recreation Center. It has memorabilia from North Carolina military history, with emphasis on the Civil War, as well as displays of modern military hardware. These include a U.S. helicopter, tank and artillery from the Vietnam era and Gulf War, and a captured Soviet-made Iraqi tank.

Hours: Noon-5 p.m., daily June through August, Wed-Sun in April, May, September and October; Sat-Sun only, November through March. Free. Fort Fisher Boulevard, Kure Beach. 251-7325.

This howitzer is among hardware at N.C. Military History Museum.

Wilmington Children's Museum

This interactive museum offers activities and exhibits to help children learn through play. Play areas include a medical center, dress-up theater, grocery store, pirate ship, water room and computer room.

Hours: 10 a.m. to 5 p.m. Tues–Sat, open Mondays in June, July and August and most school holidays. $3.50. 1020 Market St. 254-353.

DUPLIN TOURISM
The Cowan Museum and nearby Liberty Hall are in Kenansville, a short side trip off Interstate 40.

Cowan Museum

In Kenansville, an hour north of Wilmington and a short side trip off I-40, is the Cowan Museum, which displays a hands-on collection of unique and unusual artifacts from early American history. (910) 296-2149.

Hours: 10 a.m.-4 p.m. Tuesday through Saturday, 2-4 p.m. Sunday, closed Mondays and major holidays.

Depot Museum

In Lake Waccamaw, 40 minutes west of Wilmington, this small museum features exhibits the history, culture and wildlife of Columbus County, including the Waccamaw-Siouan Indians and the swamp settlement at Crusoe Island. 201 Flemington St.

Hours: 10 a.m.-3 p.m. Wednesday, Thursday and Friday; 1-3 p.m. Sunday. (910) 646-1992.

Louise Wells Cameron Art Museum

This new building houses the collection formerly known as the St. John's Museum of Art, at South 17th Street and Independence Boulevard.

SEE complete article on page 50.

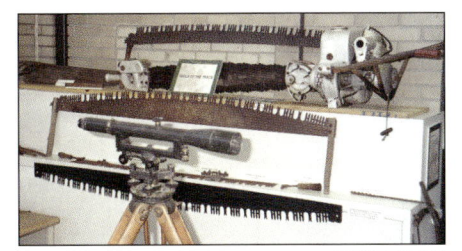

www.wilmingtontoday.com

JOHN MEYER
Logging tools at Museum of Forestry

N.C. Museum of Forestry

Exhibits on the history of North Carolina's forests starting with the Colonial naval stores industry that gave the state its "Tar Heel" nickname. In Whiteville, 50 minutes west of Wilmington. Satellite of N.C. Museum of Natural Sciences in Raleigh.

Hours: 9 a.m.-5 p.m. Mon.-Fri., 1-4 p.m. Sat., 2-5 p.m. Sun. Free. 415 S. Madison St., Whiteville. 914-4185.

Historic cemeteries

History and art meet in Wilmington's old graveyards. Tombstones from Colonial times fill the St. James churchyard at Market and Fourth streets. In the 19th Century, new cemeteries opened: Oakdale, resting place of Confederate soldiers and many leading citizens, on North 15th Street; Pine Forest, for African-Americans, on North 16th Street; and the National Cemetery for Union war dead on Market Street at 21st.

A brochure with directions to some of Oakdale's most interesting monuments is available at the cemetery office. 520 N. 15th St. 762-5682.

DICK PARROTT
Memorial stands over Confederate mass grave at Oakdale Cemetery

Cape Fear Museum
History, science, and fun!
Something for everyone.
910.341.4350
814 Market Street • Wilmington, NC
www.capefearmuseum.com

17

Historic sites
Battlefields and mansions

The well-preserved fortifications on Fort Fisher's land face look much as they did when Union forces attacked in 1865.

FORT FISHER

Fort Fisher was the Confederacy's last coastal stronghold. It kept the port of Wilmington open to blockade runners, which carried desperately needed supplies through the Union naval blockade. The railroad from Wilmington to Richmond was Robert E. Lee's last lifeline. That, and the need to supply William Tecumseh Sherman's army as it moved into North Carolina, made Fort Fisher's capture an essential Union war aim.

Twice the Union tried to capture the fort. The first attempt failed on Christmas Eve 1864. The second, on Jan. 14, 1865, succeeded after a massive naval bombardment and bloody hand-to-hand fighting. It was the Civil War's largest naval assault, the greatest anywhere until World War II.

Today, a portion of the fort's earthen mounds and a restored wooden palisade are on display. One artillery battery has been restored, with a working cannon. On the anniversary of the final battle each year, Civil War reenactors put on displays for visitors, firing the fort's three working cannon.

NEW VISITOR CENTER

The State Historic Site's visitor center has been completely redesigned with new interactive exhibits. A 16-foot relief map of the fort helps visitors understand the siege and battle. A nine-minute recorded narrative, with fiber-optic lighting effects, shows what happened and why.

A display of Civil-War era flags has a touch screen to explain their significance. (For example, that the famous Rebel battle flag is not the "Stars and Bars.") An exhibit on shoreline erosion shows why the fort's ocean face has mostly washed away.

Dioramas give a three-dimensional look at how the fort was built, how blockade runners passed through New Inlet, and how the Union assault finally overwhelmed the hard-fighting Southern defenders.

Dioramas help visitors visualize how fort was captured.

BLOCKADE RUNNERS

Fort Fisher was intimately connected to the blockade runners, which slipped into the safety of the Cape Fear River under the fort's guns. One that

Civil War reenactors fire a replica cannon during the anniversary of the battle. Living history encampments are held at Fort Fisher every January.

www.wilmingtontoday.com

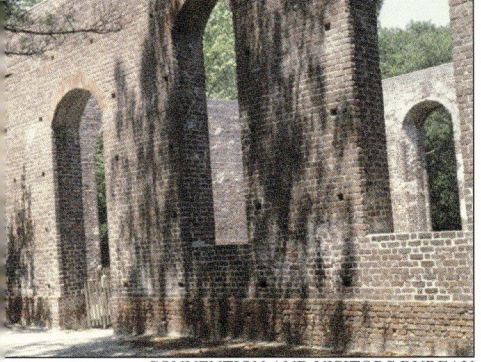

St. Philips Church, roofless for two centuries, stands at Brunswick town.

came to grief was the fast steamship *Condor*, sunk when trying to run the blockade. Its most famous passenger, the Confederate spy Rose O'Neal Greenhowe, drowned in the surf, weighed down by a sack of gold coins.

The Fort Fisher museum has a five-foot scale model of the *Condor*. This exhibit refers visitors to a companion exhibit at the nearby N.C. Aquarium, which highlights the marine life now found around the *Condor*'s wreck.

(History buffs can find Greenhowe's grave in Oakdale Cemetery on North 15th Street in Wilmington.)

SEE: N.C. Aquarium on page 22.

Hours: April-October: 9 a.m.-5 p.m. Mon-Sat, 1-5 p.m. Sun. November-March: 10 a.m.-4 p.m. Tues-Sat, 1-4 p.m. Sun. 458-5538.

To get there: U.S. 421 (Fort Fisher Boulevard) south from Kure Beach.

BRUNSWICK TOWN & FORT ANDERSON STATE HISTORIC SITE

Relics from two historical eras, Colonial and Civil War, stand side by side. This scenic site on the Cape Fear River's west bank was a thriving little seaport in the middle 1700s. Founded in 1726, it was named to flatter George I, the German-born King of England, whose lands included the

Excavated foundations of colonial Brunswick's small courthouse.

www.wilmingtontoday.com

The rattle of musketry from Colonial militia reenactors fills the woods at Moore's Creek Battlefield during anniversary observations. The visitor center's new video features these performers reenacting the battle.

German state of Brunswick.

Brunswick was rapidly eclipsed by Wilmington, which was on higher ground, farther from malarial marshes, and less exposed to hurricanes or enemy attacks. The town was attacked by Spanish privateers in 1748, hit by a hurricane in 1761, burned by the British in 1776, then abandoned.

Today, excavated ruins of Brunswick's buildings can be seen. Those foundation walls show how surprisingly small the houses, courthouse and inn were. Still impressive is St. Philips Church, the town's most substantial structure, whose thick walls have stood for two and a half centuries.

CIVIL WAR FORT

During the Civil War, the Confederates built a large earthwork, Fort Anderson, over much of the Brunswick Town site. A companion to the larger Fort Fisher on the Cape Fear's east bank, Fort Anderson was part of Wilmington's defenses. Abandoned under Union pressure soon after Fort Fisher fell in 1865, its massive earthworks are well preserved and the site for Civil War re-enactments each February.

The site's newly renovated visitor center has displays from both Colonial and Civil War periods. These include a cannon, found in the river, believed to come from a Spanish ship that blew up during the 1748 privateer attack.

Hours: 10 a.m.-4 p.m. Tues-Sat, closed Sundays and Mondays.

To get there: U.S. 17-74-76 west to N.C. 133 (Leland-Southport) exit. Left (south) on N.C. 133. Watch for signs for Orton Plantation and Brunswick Town. Turn left on St. Philips Road; follow road to end.

8887 St. Philips Rd. SE, off N.C. 133, Winnabow. 371-6613.

'Loyalists' demonstrate broadswords used by Scots at Moore's Creek.

MOORE'S CREEK NATIONAL BATTLEFIELD

This national park, about 20 miles from Wilmington, preserves an important Revolutionary War site. Moore's Creek foiled British plans to quell the rebellion in the South in 1776. It would be five years before the British returned in force to the Carolinas.

Visitors can tour the battlefield on a paved pathway that forms a three-quarter-mile loop. It includes a reconstruction of the bridge that was the battle's focus, a replica of an 18th-century cannon, and rebuilt earthworks around the Patriot camp. Along the trail are monuments, one dating from 1857, honoring fighters of both sides.

The visitor center offers a newly produced video about the battle, a diorama, and exhibits of original weapons including a flintlock musket, pistol, broadsword and swivel cannon.

Hours: 9 a.m. to 5 p.m. Closed Dec. 25.

JOHN MEYER

Visitors cross a reconstruction of the Moore's Creek Bridge. Loyalists, mostly Scots, charged across the original bridge's girders into withering Patriot fire.

To get there: U.S. 421 north to N.C. 210. Left (west) on 210 five miles to the park. From I-40: Exit 408, N.C. 210 west across U.S. 421 to the park.

200 Moores Creek Drive, off N.C. 210, Currie. (910) 284-5591.

CONVENTION & VISITORS BUREAU
Manor house at Poplar Grove.

POPLAR GROVE PLANTATION

A magnificent example of Greek Revival architecture, the house at Poplar Grove was built by the Foy family in 1850. The house is open for tours; elsewhere on the grounds are demonstrations of plantation life.

Tours: 9 a.m.-4 p.m. Mon-Sat; Noon-4 p.m. Sun. Close 5 p.m. $7 adults, $6 seniors, $3 children 6-15.

To get there: U.S. 17 north to Scotts Hill. 10200 U.S. 17. 686-9989.

THALIAN HALL

Wilmington's City Hall shares a building with a grand theater, Thalian Hall. It was built between 1855 and 1858, largely by skilled African-American craftsmen, both slave and free. The theater has hosted many famous performers and public figures.

In the 1930s, part of City Hall's north wall collapsed, encouraging "progressive" voices to call for the old building's demolition. Wilmington's innate conservatism served it well, though, and this priceless treasure was preserved.

Thalian Hall remains a centerpiece of the region's arts community. The theater is open for self-guided tours during box office hours. Donations are requested.

102 N. 3rd St; 763-3660.

SEE: Theater on page 54.

BURGWIN-WRIGHT HOUSE MUSEUM

This mansion was built in 1770 on the foundation of an old jail. The house, kitchen and gardens are a museum of daily life in the late 1700s.

In 1781, between the battles of Guilford Courthouse and Yorktown, the British General, Lord Cornwallis, used the house as his headquarters.

Tours: 10 a.m. to 3 p.m. Tues-Sat. Close at 4 p.m. Closed January. $7 adults, $3 children 12 and under.

224 Market St. 762-0570.

DICK PARROTT

BELLAMY MANSION

Built on the eve of the Civil War, the Bellamy Mansion has been restored as a museum of history and design arts. It is a spectacular example

DICK PARROTT
Rear garden gate, kitchen and Burgwin-Wright house.

of antebellum architecture. It was Union Army headquarters in 1865.

Visitors will see all four floors and the rooftop belvedere of the 22-room house. Tours begin in the reconstructed carriage house. Awaiting restoration are the original slave quarters.

Tours: On the hour from 10 a.m. to 4 p.m. Tues-Sat, 1-4 p.m. Sun. Close at 5 p.m. $7 adults, $3 children 5-12.

503 Market Street. 251-3700.

DICK PARROTT

LATIMER HOUSE

This Victorian Italianate style home in Wilmington is headquarters for the Lower Cape Fear Historical Society. Tour guides show the home and gardens and tell stories of its history.

Tours: 10 a.m.-3:30 p.m. Mon-Fri, Noon-5 p.m. Sat. Closed Sunday. $7 adults, $3 school-age children. 126 S. 3rd St. 762-0492.

20   www.wilmingtontoday.com

Battleship U.S.S. North Carolina

No visit to Wilmington is complete without a tour of our largest, heaviest and most formidably armed attraction: the battleship *U.S.S. North Carolina*.

First of a new generation of fast battleships, *North Carolina* participated in every major campaign of World War II in the Pacific.

Saved from scrapping in 1960 by a statewide fund-raising campaign, the battleship is open for tours year-round.

The tour route takes visitors from deep in the engine rooms to high up on the bridge. Highlights include:

♦ The 16-inch gun turrets that gave the ship its deadly punch. They could hurl a one-ton shell 23 miles.

♦ Steam turbines packing 120,000 horsepower that moved the ship up to 28 knots.

♦ Electronic fire-control rooms packed with radar gear and huge analog computers.

♦ A rare Kingfisher floatplane. The type did artillery spotting and rescue work for the Navy's battleships.

♦ Crew quarters, including officers' cabins, packed bunk spaces, heads, and mess halls, home to 2,339 fighting men during months at sea.

♦ Machine shops, laundry, kitchen, hospital, ship's store, post office, theater: all the facilities needed to keep a floating city functioning.

Exhibits along the tour provide context and background.

NOTE: Much of the tour requires climbing steep staircases. Only the main deck is handicapped-accessible.

Hours: 8 a.m.-8 p.m. May 16-Sept. 15; 8 a.m.-5 p.m. Sept. 16-May 15.

Admission: $9 adults, $8 seniors, $4 children 6 & over, 5 & under free.

U.S. 421 north. 350-1817.

BATTLESHIP NORTH CAROLINA
The battleship is painted in a wartime camouflage pattern. The ship arrived in Wilmington 40 years ago.

BATTLESHIP NORTH CAROLINA
Anti-aircraft batteries defended against attacking Kamikaze planes.

BATTLESHIP NORTH CAROLINA
The ship's bridge was the captain's command center when at sea.

The Historic District

After World War II, Wilmington's fine old houses were in decline. The old neighborhoods were no longer fashionable. But there was little money to replace old buildings, as happened in so many other cities. In the '60s, a threat to tear down the city's oldest house galvanized the community to protect its incomparable architectural heritage. Today, a Historic Preservation Commission and the Residents of Old Wilmington are guardians of this beautifully preserved district. It lies mainly south and east of the downtown business district.

A variety of guided tours – on foot, by horse-drawn carriage and by replica trolleys – feature the area's history and architecture.

SEE: Tours on page 26.

CAPE FEAR COAST CONVENTION & VISITORS BUREAU

DICK PARROTT

Both, DICK PARROTT

Historic District vignettes: left, a Queen Ann house. Below, fountain in yard at the Latimer House and a garden gate on South Third Street. Opposite: 1739 Smith-Anderson House, saved from demolition in the 1960s, is Wilmington's oldest building.

www.wilmingtontoday.com

CONVENTION & VISITORS BUREAU
Sharks and other large predatory fish congregate around undersea rock ledges in the Cape Fear Shoals exhibit.

Aquarium
Life in Cape Fear waters

The new North Carolina Aquarium at Fort Fisher takes visitors on a virtual journey down the Cape Fear River, from freshwater streams and swamps to tidelands, reefs and open ocean.

The aquarium, near the river's mouth, is among the region's newest and largest attractions. With a major new building and complete interior renovations, it reopened in 2002 after two years of construction.

Arriving visitors will make a dramatic entrance into the new Cape Fear Conservatory, a huge glass-roofed, tree-filled atrium full of freshwater habitats. Frogs, snakes, turtles and freshwater fish such as bass, catfish and perch are on display in a series of tanks. These represent a waterfall near the Cape Fear's Piedmont headwaters, deep holes harboring large predators, blackwater cypress swamp, tidal creeks, and the unique Carolina Bay wetlands. Along the Carolina Bay's banks are carnivorous plants common in the Cape Fear River region: pitcher plant, sundew, and venus' flytrap.

Venus' flytrap is native to the Cape Fear region.

A large exhibit features American alligators, which are native to our region and common in area swamps.

NORTH CAROLINA AQUARIUM
Divers in the Cape Fear Shoals tank use special audio equipment to answer questions from visitors.

22

www.wilmingtontoday.com

SALTWATER HABITATS

♦ **Coquina outcrop** touch pool offers hands-on learning about sea urchins, starfish, horseshoe crabs, whelks and other creatures.

♦ **Salt marsh** and **juvenile loggerhead turtle** exhibits give an up-close look at creatures that breed on or behind the beaches.

♦ **Seahorse and pipefish tank.**

♦ **Cape Fear Shoals**, a 24-foot-deep tank, gives multi-level views of large fish congregating around offshore ledges. These include sharks, barracuda, grouper, tuna, mackerel, and moray eels as well as loggerhead turtles. Several times a day, divers in this tank will speak with visitors on the dry side of the 14-foot-high viewing windows.

♦ **Open Oceans Gallery** shows creatures and habitats found off the North Carolina coast, including hardbottom reefs and the wreckage of a sunken Civil War vessel.

♦ **Masonboro Inlet jetty**, showing fish common around a wave-washed rock jetty.

♦ **Skate and ray tank**, a sandy-bottom habitat also featuring small bonnethead sharks.

VISITOR BASICS

The 2002 expansion converted a popular but modest facility, built in 1976, into a leading regional attraction. It displays more than 250 animal species and more than 2,500 individual specimens.

This is one of three state aquariums, each focusing on the environments of its own region. Others are at Manteo on the Outer Banks, and in Pine Knoll Shores on Bogue Banks, near Morehead City.

Hours: 9 a.m.-5 p.m. daily. Closed Thanksgiving, Christmas and New Year's Day. $6 adults, $5 seniors and active military, $4 children 6-17. 458-8257.

To get there: Follow U.S. 421 south from Kure Beach. Just past the Fort Fisher State Historic Site, turn left on Loggerhead Road, past the beach access. From Southport, take ferry to Fort Fisher; north on 421, right on Loggerhead Road.

Angelfish (left) and porgy are among the many colorful inhabitants of the offshore hard-bottom habitat.

Touch pool encourages visitors of all ages to investigate seashore creatures.

www.wilmingtontoday.com

Ferry Schedule

Leave Southport	Leave Fort Fisher	Leave Southport	Leave Fort Fisher
a.m.	a.m.	p.m.	p.m.
5:30	--	12:15	12:15
--	6:15	1:00	1:00
7:00	--	1:45	1:45
*7:45	7:45	2:30	2:30
8:30	*8:30	3:15	3:15
9:15	9:15	4:00	4:00
10:00	10:00	4:45	4:45
10:45	10:45	--	5:30
11:30	11:30	6:15	--
		--	7:00
		**7:45	--
		--	**8:30

* Winter only: to May 18, Sept. 9 and after
** Summer only: May 19–Sept. 8

Cape Fear Ferry

Two of the Cape Fear Coast's favorite destinations – Fort Fisher and Southport – are just a few minutes apart as the gull flies, but separated by the wide mouth of the Cape Fear River. To save a drive of nearly two hours, and enjoy a beautiful scenic cruise besides, try the state ferry.

The ride takes about 25 minutes and offers excellent views of the river, tidal marshes and lighthouses, North Carolina's oldest, newest, and smallest. Southeast, on Bald Head Island, is "Old Baldy," built in 1817. Southwest is Oak Island light, built in 1958. Along the west bank, near the Southport ferry terminal, is the little Price's Creek light, a river channel beacon from the 1800s.

NOTE: The ferry may not run during high wind or fog.

One-way tolls are:
Car and passengers, **$5**
Car & trailer over 20 feet, **$10**
Motorcycle and riders, **$3**
Bicycle and rider, **$2**
Pedestrian, **$1**

One other ferry crosses the Cape Fear River, well upstream. For details: SEE: Daytrips on page 60.

www.wilmingtontoday.com

Getting around
Traffic and transportation

As the city has grown, Wilmington's traffic has outgrown its highways. The Martin Luther King, Jr. Parkway will be finished, and the first stretch of the I-140 Outer Loop Freeway will open, in 2005. (Maps, pages 24 & 56.)

To minimize aggravation in driving around town, here are some tips:

♦ **Red-light runners.** Local drivers are bad about this. To protect yourself, look twice before going on green to be sure some knucklehead isn't trying to race through on the yellow.

♦ **Turn-signal phobia.** For some reason, many Wilmington drivers don't seem to know what to do with those levers on their steering columns. Keep that in mind, and keep the rest of us in mind too: Please use *your* turn signals when changing lanes, and especially before making left turns.

♦ **Slow ride in the fast lane.** We love sight-seers. But if you aren't sure where you're going, please stay in the right lane as you look. Our traffic arteries are clogged enough without slow-moving cars blocking the passing lane.

DICK PARROTT

♦ **Summertime stack-up:** Until our two bypass highways are finished in 2005, most west-bound traffic from I-40 and U.S. 17 is funneled into Market Street. It's then shunted onto one-way streets for the last leg out of town. On busy days, the line waiting to turn onto 16th Street can back up for blocks. If you're heading for the Cape Fear Memorial Bridge, stay in the right lane on Market (it's U.S. 17 Business) and head straight on Downtown.

Trust us: the traffic will be lighter, and the drive's more interesting, too. Even if you aren't tempted to stop Downtown (and you ought to), this is an easy alternate route to the bridge. Turn left on Third or Front streets; either takes you directly to the bridge's on-ramps, and through the beautiful heart of the Historic District.

♦ **Left-turn hangups:** Some busy corners don't have turn lanes. If you're in a line of 20 cars behind the one waiting to turn left, you may have to wait through an entire cycle before you can move ahead.

Stick to the right lane as you approach these spots. The worst of them are on the narrow stretch of Market Street at 17th Street, 23rd Street and Forest Hills Drive, and on Wrightsville Avenue at Colonial and Country Club.

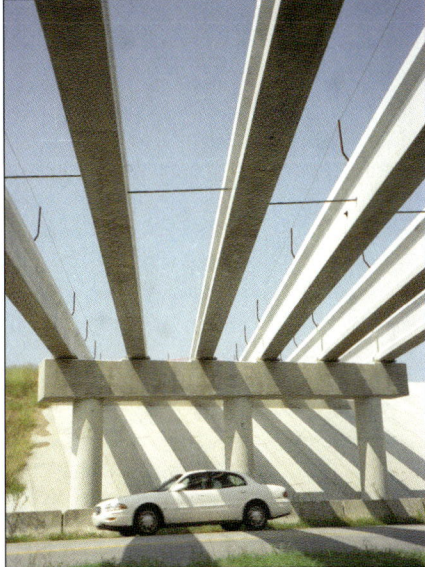

DICK PARROTT
Smile, you're on red-light camera. Many busy intersections use this system.

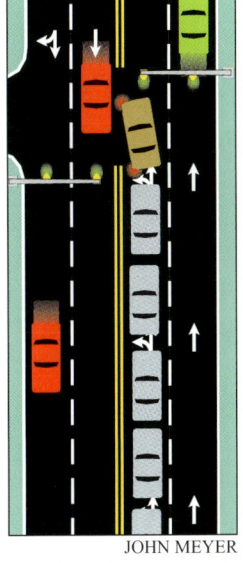

JOHN MEYER
Don't get stuck.

JOHN MEYER
Interstate 140 will help Brunswick County beach-bound travelers avoid Wilmington traffic, starting 2005

Travel guide on line
For maps, route advice and tips on what to look for along the way, see our web site at www.wilmingtontoday.com
For attractions within a two-hour drive, see Day Trips on page 60.

JOHN MEYER
Martin Luther King, Jr. Parkway leapfrogs wetlands. Bypass opens in 2005.

www.wilmingtontoday.com

Tours
Afloat, on wheels, on foot

Civic boosters once called Wilmington "The Port City of Progress and Pleasure." Corny, sure, but we think it's still true.

There are few pleasures greater than cruising the Cape Fear River or other waterways.

Henrietta III:

A dramatic presence on the downtown waterfront, the cruise boat *Henrietta III* offers daily sight-seeing trips and lunch and dinner cruises.

Built in 1985, it once cruised the Mississippi River as a casino riverboat. It came to Wilmington in 2000. The boat's new name recalls *Henrietta II*, a smaller stern-wheeler that plied the Cape Fear from 1988 through 1999.

The original *Henrietta* was launched in 1818, the dawn of steam-powered travel on the Cape Fear.

Henrietta III is North Carolina's largest riverboat and has an elevator to make all decks fully accessible.

Scheduled cruises around Wrightsville Beach, charters and expeditions to Masonboro Island are offered by cruise line based at Wrightsville Beach.

The main salon seats 228 dinner guests. The second deck, formerly the casino, seats an additional 144. Both levels have large dance floors.

The top level has both glass-topped and open-air decks giving panoramic views of the river and waterfront.

Sight-seeing cruises: 90 minutes, noon and 2:30 p.m., Tues-Sun, April-October. $10 adults, $5 children 2-12.

Lunch cruises: 90 minutes, noon Tues-Sun. $18 adults, $10 children.

Dinner cruises: Wednesday and Thursday buffet: 6:30-8:30 p.m. June-August. $27 adults, $17 children.

Friday buffet dinner dance: 7:30-10 p.m. April-December. $33 adults, $23 children; Saturday buffet dinner dance: 6:30-9:30 p.m. April-December. $36 adults, $26 children.

Paid reservations required for meal cruises. Water at Dock. 343-1611.

Captain J.N. Maffit

This former U.S. Navy launch has been cruising the Cape Fear River for 25 years. It is named for Capt. John Newland Maffit. A Wilmingtonian, he left the U.S. Navy when the Civil War started and commanded the Confederate raider *C.S.S. Florida*, which wreaked havoc with Yankee shipping.

The *Maffit* conducts 45-minute narrated sightseeing cruises and a river taxi service between downtown and the Battleship North Carolina.

Cruises: 11 a.m. and 3 p.m. daily Memorial Day through Labor Day. Weekends only during May and September through mid-December. $8 adults, $4 children 2-12.

Departs from Riverfront Park, Market and Water streets. 343-1611.

ENJOY A RIVERBOAT CRUISE!

Narrated Sightseeing Cruises
Dinner Dance Cruises
Sunset Cruises
Private Party Cruises
Luncheon Cruises
Wedding Cruises

aboard North Carolina's Largest Riverboat

HENRIETTA III
UP TO 600 PASSENGERS   3 PRIVATE DECKS
GIFT CERTIFICATES

Cape Fear Riverboats, Inc. • P.O. Box 1881 • Wilmington, NC
(910) 343-1611 • (800) 676-0162 • www.cfrboats.com

CAPE FEAR RIVERBOATS

The 'Henrietta III' is named for an early Cape Fear steamboat.

'Captain J.N.Maffit' has cruised the Cape Fear River since 1977, now runs river taxi service.

RIVER TAXI

The *Maffit* departs from Riverfront Park on the quarter hour and from the Battleship on the hour and half hour except at 11:30 a.m. and 3:30 p.m., during Sightseeing Cruises. $2, children under 2 free. 343-1611.

WRIGHTSVILLE BEACH SCENIC CRUISES

Explore the waters around Wrightsville Beach on a spacious restroom-equipped pontoon boat. Offerings range from one-hour narrated harbor cruises and sunset trips, to Masonboro Island expeditions and nature excursions with a marine biologist as guide. Motor boat rentals and motor yacht charters are also available.

Hours: Harbor cruises depart at 11 a.m. and 1:30 p.m.; sunset cruise departs an hour and a half before sunset, or between 6 p.m. and 6:30 p.m. Masonboro Island shuttle departs 11 a.m. with pickup at 1 p.m. Cruises depart opposite the Blockade Runner Hotel, 275 Waynick Blvd. 350-2628.

WINNER CRUISE BOATS

Based at Carolina Beach Marina, this company's boats offer scenic, moonlight and dinner cruises, as well as large boats for offshore fishing.

1 Carl Winner Drive, Carolina Beach. 458-5356.

CAROLINA COASTAL ADVENTURES

Boat trips to Masonboro and other uninhabited islands, bird-watching expeditions, lighthouse tours, picnics and sunset cruises, all with licensed captains. Also inshore and offshore fishing trips. This company is affiliated

• PIZZA PARTIES • FAMILY PICNICS • NATURE EXCURSIONS •

Blockade Runner

Wrightsville Beach SCENIC CRUISES

Boats available all year for special charters

Pontoon Boat
- Narrated Harbor & Sunset Cruises
- Shuttles to Masonboro Island
- Nature Excursions w/ Marine Biologist

Lady Star ~ 40' Luxury Motor Yacht
For Charter by Hour or Day
- OR -
See the waterway on your own!
Rent a boat for the day! ~ Fun & Easy

Lady Star

17' Boat For Rent

Call for Schedule & Prices
350-BOAT (2628)
www.cruiseinc.net

• COCKTAIL PARTIES • FAMILY REUNIONS • FIELD TRIPS •

Fishing
Inshore, Nearshore, Offshore

Kayaking
Tours, Lessons, Rentals

Boating
Sightseeing, Birding, Water Taxi

910-458-9111

Carolina Coastal Adventures, Capt. John's Fishing Charters & Kayak Carolina

Adventure Supply Store, Bike Rentals, Walking & Biking Tours, Kids Camps, Groups

*1337 Bridge Barrier Road
Carolina Beach, NC*

---

www.wilmingtontoday.com

Kayak Carolina offers close-up access to salt marshes. Canoes and pedal boats are for rent at Greenfield Lake.

with Kayak Carolina. 458-9111

KAYAK CAROLINA

This Carolina Beach-based company offers guided nature tours and educational programs, as well as kayak rentals. Guides are interpretive naturalists, experienced paddlers, and certified in first aid and CPR. Two, four and six-hour, all-day and overnight tours are offered.

Options include coastal marshlands, the Intracoastal Waterway, Cape Fear River and other area waterways, with trips to Zeke's Island, Masonboro Island and Hutaff Island.

Basic two-hour tour includes introductory paddling and safety lesson. $35 adults, half price children 11 and under. 1331 Bridge Barrier Road, Carolina Beach. 458-9111.

GREENFIELD LAKE BOATS

A great way to appreciate this garden spot in the heart of Wilmington is from the water. Canoes and pedal-powered paddle boats are available for rent from a concession operated by Cape Fear River Watch.

Hours: 11 a.m.-6 p.m. seasonally. Canoes or paddle boat rentals $8 first hour, $6 each additional hour.

Fifth Avenue and Willard Street. 341-7868 or 762-5606.

SUNDOWN CHARTERS

Outings to Masonboro Island and other beaches, waterway cruises and offshore fishing are offered by this Coast Guard-licensed captain. 793-6262 or 612-5162.

SEE: Fishing on page 46.

WILMINGTON TROLLEY

A 45-minute narrated tour of the Historic District on a trolley-style bus. The route follows the scenic Cape Fear River waterfront with stops at major historic landmarks, mansions and museums. Get on or off at any stop on the route; tickets sold on board and

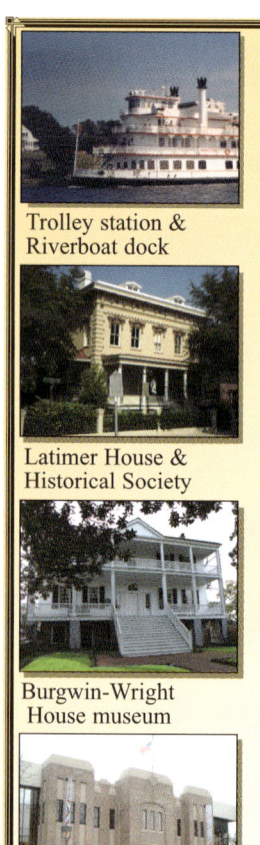

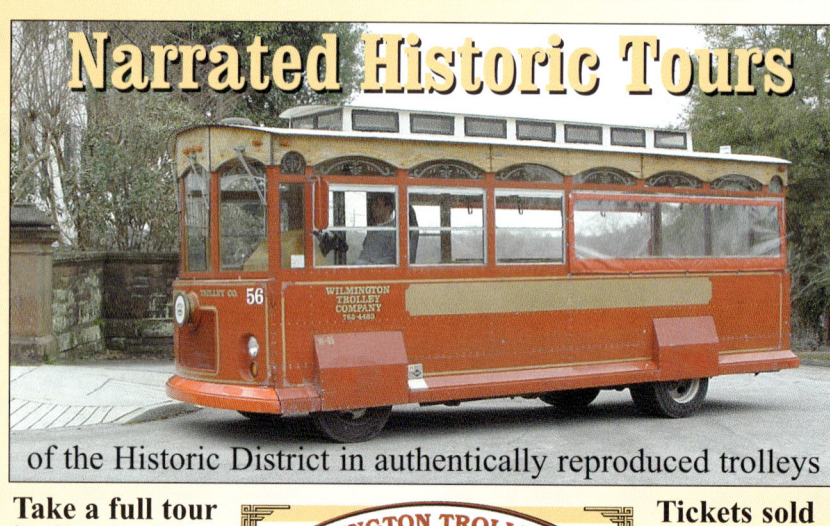

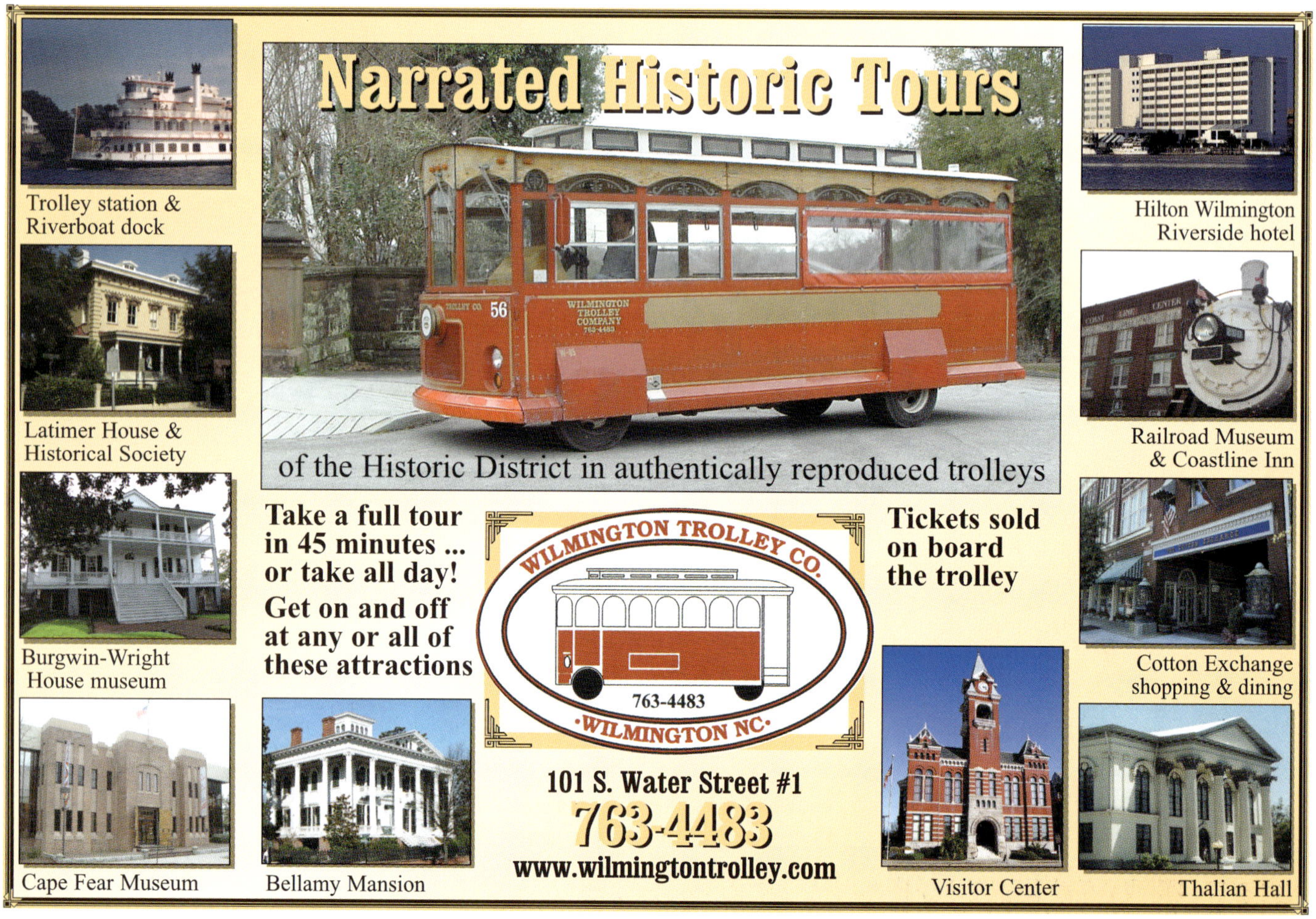

Narrated Historic Tours

of the Historic District in authentically reproduced trolleys

Trolley station & Riverboat dock

Latimer House & Historical Society

Burgwin-Wright House museum

Cape Fear Museum

Bellamy Mansion

Hilton Wilmington Riverside hotel

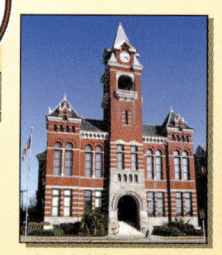

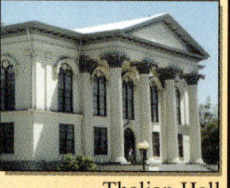

Railroad Museum & Coastline Inn

Cotton Exchange shopping & dining

Visitor Center

Thalian Hall

Take a full tour in 45 minutes ... or take all day!

Get on and off at any or all of these attractions

Tickets sold on board the trolley

WILMINGTON TROLLEY CO.
763-4483
·WILMINGTON NC·

101 S. Water Street #1
763-4483
www.wilmingtontrolley.com

Wilmington Trolley runs narrated tours of the Historic District.

good for an entire round trip.

Stops include the Latimer House, Burgwin-Wright House, Cape Fear Museum, Bellamy Mansion, Old Courthouse, Thalian Hall, The Cotton Exchange, Coastline Inn & Railroad Museum, and Hilton hotel.

Times: Hourly, 10 a.m.-5 p.m., April-October. $10 adults, $5 children 2-12. Water and Dock streets, at *Henrietta III* wharf. 763-4483.

A free shuttle trolley also operates downtown. SEE: Downtown, page 7.

Studio entrance on 23rd Street.

EUE/SCREEN GEMS STUDIO TOUR

EUE/Screen Gems Studio is the largest working movie-production facility east of California.

It was established in 1984 by Dino DiLaurentiis but has changed ownership twice. It now covers 32 acres with nine sound stages, a back lot and post-production facilities.

The studio is open for guided tours on Saturdays and Sundays, weather permitting. This walking tour includes access to some sets, depending on production schedules.

Times: 11 a.m. Wed-Fri., 10 a.m., noon and 2 p.m., Sat., noon & 2 p.m. Sun. Mid-May-August. Reduced schedules Spring & Fall. $10 adults, $5 seniors and children.

1223 N. 23rd St. 343-3433.

CARRIAGE TOURS

Tour the downtown waterfront and Historic District at a leisurely pace, with narration by costumed drivers. Tours are in a one-horse carriage, or a two-horse replica of the horse-drawn streetcars that once served as Wilmington's public transit system.

Seasonal tours include a "haunted" Halloween ride and Christmas and Valentine's tours in a closed carriage.

Times: 10 a.m.-10 p.m. Tues-Sat, 11 a.m.-4 p.m. April-October. Limited schedules November-March. $9 adults, $4 children under 12.

Market at Water. 251-8889.

FORT FISHER STATE RECREATION AREA

Park rangers offer a summer series of guided nature walks. Subjects include birds, shells, surf fishing, sea turtles and wetland life. For details, call park office. U.S. 421 south. 458-5798.

Replica of 19th-century horse-drawn streetcar is used for Downtown tours.

'Dawson's Creek' cast on a mural at EUE/Screen Gems studios.

THE MOVIE BUSINESS

Feature films: This is a partial list of titles made in the Wilmington area since the middle 1980s.

The Bedroom Window
Betsy's Wedding
Billy Bathgate
Black Dog
Black Knight
Blue Velvet
Cat's Eye
Crimes of the Heart
The Crow
The Dangerous Lives of Altar Boys
Divine Secrets of the Ya-ya Sisterhood
Domestic Disturbance
Elmo in Grouchland
Firestarter
The Hudsucker Proxy
I Know What You Did Last Summer
King Kong Lives
Lolita
Maximum Overdrive
Morgan's Ferry
Muppets From Space
Rambling Rose
Raw Deal
The Road to Wellville
Sleeping With the Enemy
Summer Catch
Super Mario Brothers
Teenage Mutant Ninja Turtles II
28 Days
Virus
A Walk to Remember
Weekend at Bernie's
Year of the Dragon

TV: In addition to numerous made-for-TV movies, pilots and cable shows, several TV series have been filmed here, including the current WB hit *Dawson's Creek*.

American Gothic
Dawson's Creek
Matlock
The Young Indiana Jones Chronicles

Shorts: The Wilmington studios, and the many skilled film-industry craftsmen who work here, have also produced innumerable commercials, short films and music videos.

Info: Wilmington Regional Film Commission, 343-3456

Greenfield Tours

Cape Fear River Watch conducts eco-tours of this former mill-pond and surrounding woods and wetlands.

Times: 9 a.m. Sat. South Fifth at Willard. 341-7868 or 762-5606.

Tours by Degrees

Local history experts specialize in historical and cultural tours for groups, including conventions and bus tours. Their expertise includes art, antiques architecture and they can address any aspect of the area's history.

Ed Turberg is an architectural historian; Janet Seapker is retired director of the Cape Fear Museum in Wilmington. 762-6301.

Ghosts of the South

A 90-minute living history tour Downtown. By reservation. 297-6183.

Times: 7 and 9 p.m. $9 adults, $5 children. Market at Front.

Walking Tours of Old Wilmington

Downtown and Historic District tours, 90 minutes to two hours. Reservations required. 602-6055

Times: 10 a.m. daily, 1 p.m. Tues-Sat; 6:30 p.m. Fri-Sat, 8:30 p.m. nightly. $12 adults, $10 seniors and students. Under 7, free. Market at Water.

Wilmington Adventure Tour

Longtime Wilmington resident Bob Jenkins, the man with the straw hat and walking cane, offers colorful tales of Wilmington's past. Two hours.

Times: 10 a.m. & 2 p.m. April-Oct. $10. Market at Water. 763-1785.

Old Wilmington by Candlelight Tour

This annual Christmas-time event is a fund-raiser for the Lower Cape Fear Historical Society, which operates the Latimer House museum.

The tour takes visitors into a dozen or more of Wilmington's finest old houses, decorated for the holidays.

Dates: Dec. 6 and 7, 2003.

Times: 4-8 p.m. Saturday, 2-6 p.m. Sunday. $20. 762-0492.

CONVENTION & VISITORS BUREAU
Bob Jenkins offers his own unique perspective on Old Wilmington in Wilmington Adventure Tours.

Garden Tours

Our best-known public gardens have beautiful blossoms on display from March through November.

Airlie Gardens

Established as a private preserve by railroad baron Pembroke Jones and his wife, this coastal garden was acquired by New Hanover County in 1998. ("Keeping up with the Joneses" originally referred to Airlie's first owners.) Featured are freshwater lakes, a rain garden, and of course azaleas galore. The gardens border the marshes of Bradley Creek, home to wading birds, waterfowl and other wildlife.

Hours: April 28-Oct. 27, tickets sold 9 a.m.-4 p.m. Fri-Sat, 1-4 p.m. Sun. Close 5 p.m. Spring schedule: March 22-April 28, open Tues-Sun. $8 adults, $7 seniors, $2 children. Discount for local residents. 793-7531

Oleander Drive to Airlie Road; one mile to entrance.

Arboretum

The New Hanover County Cooperative Extension Service, with help from a small army of green-thumbed volunteers, has developed a public arboretum at the corner of Oleander Drive and Greenville Loop Road. It demonstrates landscaping ideas and techniques for species that thrive in our climate.

Free admission. **Hours:** 8:30 a.m. to 5 p.m. daily. Oleander Drive at Greenville Loop Road. 452-6393

Greenfield Gardens

This city park around Greenfield Lake was established in the 1930s. Plantings here inspired the Azalea Festival, starting in 1948. Under towering cypress and wisteria-draped pines, the azaleas are the headliner attraction with a supporting cast including camellia, dogwood, redbud, crape myrtle and magnolia.

Greenfield Park has picnic areas, a five-mile lakeshore trail, Fragrance Garden, amphitheater, skate park, canoe, paddle boat and bike rentals.

South Fifth Avenue at Willard, off Third. Lake Shore Drive circles the lake. 341-7868

JOHN MEYER
Greenfield at azalea time

Orton Plantation Gardens

This former rice plantation on the Cape Fear River's west bank includes one of the region's oldest houses, the original rooms of which were built in 1725. The house is not open for tours. The 20 acres of gardens have been a showplace for nearly a century. Visitors can enjoy a grand vista over the river and the marshes that once grew rice. Near Brunswick Town/Fort Anderson historic site.

Hours: Open 8 a.m. daily March-August; 10 a.m. September through November. Closed December through February. $8 adults, $7 seniors, $3 children. 371-6851

Orton Road: N.C. 133 12 miles south of U.S. 17-74-76.

Azalea Festival Tours

Every April, the city's finest gardens are open just as the flowering shrubs are at their peak. 11 gardens, including Airlie, are featured. A separate Homes Tour features eight houses in the Historic District.

Gardens: 10:30 a.m.-6 p.m. Thurs-Sun, April 4-6. $10. **Homes:** 1-6 p.m. April 5-6. Tickets $20, 5725 Oleander Drive. 794-4650

PAULINE PURDUM
Wisteria at Arboretum

Festivals
Events and celebrations

AZALEA FESTIVAL
The North Carolina Azalea Festival at Wilmington started in 1948 to showcase the brilliant floral displays with which our town greets the spring.

Concerts, a parade, a street fair with food, crafts and entertainment and a garden tour are highlights.

The 2003 festival begins **Wednesday, April 2** and runs through **Sunday, April 6.** The concert, with Al Green, begins at 8 p.m. April 2 in Trask Coliseum. A second concert will feature Country act Lonestar on Friday.

Tickets are sold for bleacher seats at the Saturday parade and for garden and home tours. Ticket office: 5725 Oleander Drive, Unit B7. 794-4650.

COASTAL CAROLINA AIR SHOW
Wilmington International Airport is the setting for this celebration of the 100th anniversary of powered flight, culminating with a flight by the Air Force Thunderbirds precision flying team. **April 12-13.** 772-7983

STRAWBERRY FESTIVAL
The town of Chadbourn, an hour from Wilmington, celebrates this favorite fruit it once shipped north by the trainload. Worth a detour off U.S. 74 for a beach-bound traveler. **May 1-5.**

Calendar and weather online
www.WilmingtonToday.com

CAPE FEAR COAST CONVENTION & VISITORS BUREAU
Azalea Festival garden party features Azalea Belles celebrating spring flowers.

JOE STANLEY for SOUTHPORT-OAK ISLAND CofC

FOURTH OF JULY FESTIVAL
The North Carolina Fourth of July Festival takes over downtown Southport every Independence Day. A parade, food booths, crafts and entertainment fill the streets of this charming waterfront town. **July 1-4.**

NAUTICAL FESTIVAL
The Coast Guard sailing ship *Eagle* visits Downtown Wilmington. Tours, boat shows and seafood. **July 25-27.**

SHRIMP FESTIVAL
Fresh seafood is the star of this celebration at Sneads Ferry, 45 minutes northeast of Wilmington. **Aug. 9-10.**

SPOT FESTIVAL
These tasty pan fish are fried by the thousands at Hampstead's biggest annual event. U.S. 17, **Sept. 27-28.**

CONVENTION & VISITORS BUREAU

RIVERFEST
This weekend bash celebrates the Cape Fear River, centered on a street fair along Water Street. **Oct. 4-5.**

WEATHER FACTS
Signs of spring: First bulbs blossom in February. We're in USDA Zone 8.

Beach season: Water temps allow swimming May through October.

Summer: Hot and humid, but ocean's influence moderates highs. 80s and low 90s typical.

Winter: Mild, first frost in December. Typical cold days are sunny; highs in 50s and 60s common, 70s not unusual either.

Temperature extremes:
High: 104, June 27, 1952.
Low: 0, Dec. 25, 1989.

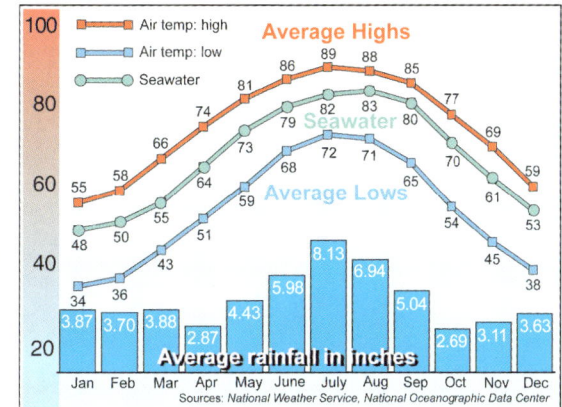

Snow: Rare. Significant accumulations only every five or six years. Record: 15 inches, Dec. 23-24, 1989.

Hurricanes: As rare as major snows, and as unpredictable. From 1960 to 1995, only one, Diana in 1984, made a direct hit. But 1996, 1998 and 1999 saw four -- Bertha, Fran, Bonnie and Floyd -- pass over Wilmington. 1997 and 2000 through 2002 were hurricane-free.

Hurricane season is June 1 through Nov. 30. Early and late storms are rare. August and September are peak season.

Hurricanes give plenty of warning. Worst case for visitors is an evacuation order and, unfortunately, an interrupted vacation, but no immediate danger except extra-heavy traffic.

www.wilmingtontoday.com

Upbeat, Casual and Delicious

Pastas/Risotto

Fresh Seafood

Beef/Mixed Grill

Sandwiches/Burritos

Smoked Fish

Daily Chef's Specials

Homemade Desserts/Breads

Largest Selection of Beer

Wines by the Glass

All ABC Permits

Check our website for daily specials:
www.tomatozrestaurant.com

GREAT LATE NIGHT LIVE MUSIC
(no cover)

Tuesday, Wednesday, and Thursday nights at 10 p.m.

Sunday: Jazz at 8 p.m.

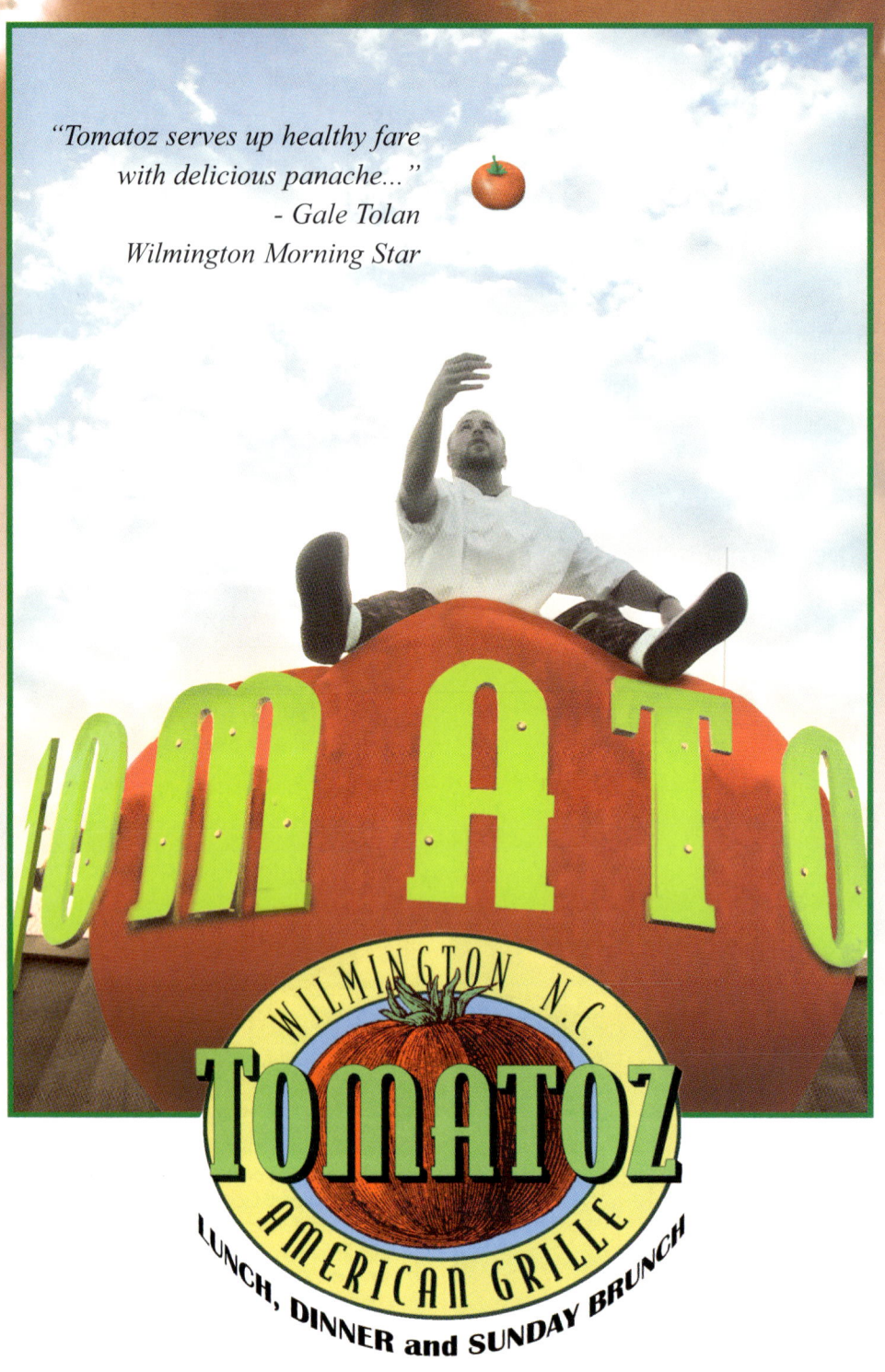

"Tomatoz serves up healthy fare with delicious panache..."
- Gale Tolan
Wilmington Morning Star

TOMATOZ
WILMINGTON N.C.
AMERICAN GRILLE
LUNCH, DINNER and SUNDAY BRUNCH

1201 S. College Road
(at the corner of South College and Wrightsville Avenue)
Call ahead seating
313-0541 • 313-0543 (fax)

Dining
A WORLD OF CHOICES

Famous for local specialties such as pork barbecue and ocean-fresh seafood, the Cape Fear Coast is also home to a broad range of fine dining.

Area restaurants feature cuisines from every corner of the world.

It wasn't so very long ago that Wilmington had very few choices for a nice dinner out. But before the boom in restaurants began, there were the native specialties. The names for these, as often as not, referred as much to a social event as to the food involved.

But, oh, the food!

Pig pickings. Oyster roasts. Shrimperoos. Fish fries and Brunswick stew.

And along with the signature dishes, the supporting cast: collard greens, hush puppies, grits, slaw, cornbread and the other staples of the Southern table.

Now that we're blessed with our choice of Thai, French, Indian and Mexican restaurants, we're also in easy reach of the traditional foods that help make this area special.

SEAFOOD

Let's start with seafood. We sometimes hear visitors claim they "don't like fish," and that usually comes down to the supposed "fishy smell." Fear not, gentle readers: fresh fish, the kind we're blessed to get, right off the boat, doesn't offend the senses.

Whether it's a traditional fish fry at a "country cooking" or soul food restaurant, or a chef's specialty in an upscale eatery, the varied and subtle flavors of seafood are among the chief glories of Cape Fear cooking.

Among the best-known commercial species are grouper, dolphin (a fish, often called "mahi-mahi" on menus to avoid confusion with the mammal), and flounder. But local boats bring ashore a large variety of other fish species, which are well worth a try. Shrimp, oysters,

RICHARD K. DAVIS

CAPE FEAR COAST CONVENTION & VISITORS BUREAU
However it's cooked, few dishes are better than shrimp fresh off the boat.

clams, scallops and blue crabs are all harvested from North Carolina waters.

But if seafood just doesn't appeal to you, remember that this corner of North Carolina is also among the world's leading producers of pork, chicken and turkey. The town of Rose Hill, less than an hour's drive up I-40, featured a long-running annual chicken festival centered on the "world's largest" frying pan.

And that brings us to a subject that inspires passions and debates of near-religious fervor.

www.wilmingtontoday.com

Barbecue

The essence of barbecue is a matter of grammar. In Eastern North Carolina, "barbecue" isn't an adjective or even a verb. It's not a style or a sauce to be applied to a piece of chicken; it's not a way to cook a steak.

It's a noun.

Barbecue refers to pit-cooked pork. In this part of the world, it's served with a vinegar-and-red-pepper sauce. While barbecue cooks have their own secret ingredients, the Eastern N.C. style doesn't include tomatoes, mustard or molasses.

There are doctrinal disputes: whether the meat should be chopped or "pulled," and over the all-important question of a wood fire or gas.

The barbecue "pit" tends now to be a metal cylinder, hinged on one side, and mounted on a trailer.

A pig picking itself is just what it sounds like. The meat, succulent and juicy, almost falls off the bone.

But it isn't necessary to attend a pig picking to experience good barbecue. A number of barbecue restaurants serve the genuine article, and some offer it ready-packed to take home. Expect a choice of traditional side dishes, especially hush puppies, slaw, collards and black-eyed peas.

Around here, barbecue is a noun, not a verb or adjective.

Oysters

Ranking right up there with a pig-picking as an unforgettable eating experience is a Carolina oyster roast.

In its simplest form, it's experienced around sawhorse tables covered with newspapers. Buckets of freshly steamed oysters are dumped in the center, and eager diners armed with shucking knives dig in, prying open the shells to get at the palate-pleasing meat and broth inside.

Melted butter, lemon and hot sauce (purists debate Tabasco versus Texas Pete brands) and cocktail sauce are the standard accompaniments.

Some restaurants are ready to approximate the oyster roast experience, taking much of the mess (and the shucking) off the diner's hands. In season, the best local oysters come from Stump Sound, Topsail Sound, and the Lockwood Folly area (near Holden Beach and Varnamtown) in southern Brunswick County.

Out of season (those non-"R" months) any fresh oysters are likely to come from the Gulf Coast. Purists will still argue there's nothing better than a mess of Stump Sound singles on a cold November night.

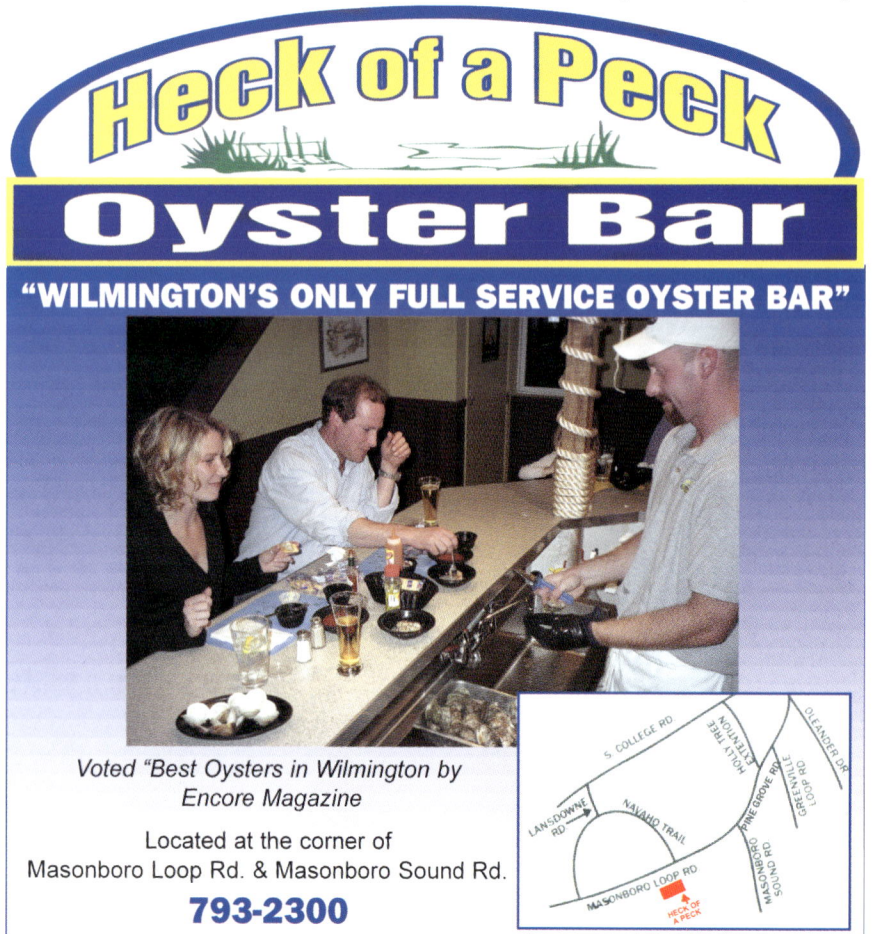

Heck of a Peck Oyster Bar

"WILMINGTON'S ONLY FULL SERVICE OYSTER BAR"

Voted "Best Oysters in Wilmington by Encore Magazine

Located at the corner of Masonboro Loop Rd. & Masonboro Sound Rd.

793-2300

The Fish Market

Open to the public.

- Fresh local seafood
- Best prices in the area
- Knowledgeable staff who will answer your questions

Enjoy the Cape Fear area's seafood bounty at The Fish Market!

**6826 Market Street
792-1447**

Restaurants
Fine dining and family fun

Many of our region's widely varied restaurants are blessed with highly trained chefs, who bring world-class standards to their kitchens.

Increasingly, finer restaurants are promoting their chefs and their signature dishes to set them apart from the competition.

Besides the food, a number of restaurants add to the dining experience with spectacular views of ocean, sound or river, or with live music.

A competitive market has kept menu prices moderate. Entrees typically range from $9 to $19, with few above $25.

Wilmington and the beaches enjoy a casual style, and few restaurants require guests to dress up for dinner.

Some restaurants take reservations during busy times, but don't for lunch or on weeknights. Many don't take reservations at all. It's always wise to check ahead.

Dining Guide

A directory of *Wilmington Today*'s restaurant advertisers, with descriptions of two of their featured entrees.

Alleigh's
4925 New Centre Drive. 793-0999

Four fabulous restaurants under one roof. Choice steaks, all-you-can-eat buffets, oyster bar, sports bar and grill and senior discounts. Kids eat free with $10 Thrill Zone PowerCard purchase. Virtual reality games, live entertainment, banquet facilities and much more.

Fried Seafood Platter: Shrimp, oysters, scallops, clam strips and fish lightly breaded and fried golden brown.

Alleigh's Chicken: Chicken breast with sauteed artichoke hearts, bell peppers, red onions and mushrooms in Montrachet sauce.

Boca Bay
2025 Eastwood Road. 256-1887

A new wine bar that focuses on tapas-style small-plate cuisine. Specializing in sushi, seafood, pasta and Thai dishes. Finish with colossal confections.

Horseradish Crusted Ribeye: With potato gratin & red wine reduction.

Bouillon of Red Snapper: With steamed vegetables over coconut rice.

Cafe Atlantique
1900 Eastwood Road. 256-0995

Featuring legendary cuisine with a warm, friendly atmosphere, Cafe Atlantique is renowned for fresh local seafood and the finest in poultry, meat and game. Nestled in beautiful Lumina Station, it is noteworthy for its eccentric wine list and superlative staff. Open for lunch Tues-Sat and dinner nightly. The menu is changed seasonally. Reservations recommended.

Jerusalem artichoke crusted Turbot with Scallions and Tarragon Jus.

Roasted Saddle of Venison with Oxtail Cannelloni and Horseradish Sabayon.

Continued on next page

Eat. Drink. Play.

Looking for a unique dining and entertainment experience?

Put Alleigh's at the top of your game plan. Our 35,000 square foot complex has everything from live bands, an outdoor Tiki Bar & Cafe and a 31 TV screen sports bar, to the *you've-got-to-see-it-to-believe-it* Thrill Zone Game Room, featuring video games, arcade games, virtual reality – even a roller coaster simulator!

And wait 'til you see the menu.

Burgers, ribs, fresh seafood, grilled filet – the choices are as varied as the games. But much tastier.

OPEN MONDAY - FRIDAY, 11:00 A.M. TO 2:00 A.M. • OPEN SATURDAY & SUNDAY, 10:00 A.M. TO 2:00 A.M.
LATE-NITE MENU TIL 1:00 A.M. • SUNDAY BRUNCH 10:00 A.M. TO 2:00 P.M.

Alleigh's
Your Game Plan for Food and Fun

4925 NEW CENTRE DRIVE • WILMINGTON • 910.793.0999

CERTIFIED ANGUS BEEF • SINCE 1978

www.wilmingtontoday.com

Dining Guide
Continued from previous page.

Cafe de France
1122 Military Cutoff Road. 256-6600

Bonjour! Dine in an authentic little corner of France. Enjoy casual French dining, cafe lunches or evening bistro in our affordable French bistro and creperie. Try our specialty wines and over 40 kinds of crepes. Open 7 days a week for lunch and dinner. Sunday brunch 10 a.m. to 2:30 p.m. Patio dining and live entertainment.

Moroccan Meatloaf: All beef, beautifully spiced, topped with a red wine cream sauce.

Crepe D'Alsace: Crepe with sausage, Swiss cheese, caramelized onions and a creamy mustard sauce.

The Cape Restaurant
535 The Cape Blvd. 794-5757

With its spacious facilities and beautiful golf course vistas, dining at The Cape is a truly rewarding experience. Open daily for lunch with an exciting dinner menu Friday nights and an elaborate all-you-can-eat Sunday brunch. Seasonal menus and awesome daily specials created by executive chef Michael Day. All ABC permits.

BROWNIE HARRIS

Thai Sate' Chicken Salad: Mixed greens, honey toasted almonds, mandarin oranges, crispy rice noodles and Thai grilled chicken, tossed with a cool tangy mandarin orange vinaigrette.

Pasta Victoria: Sauteed shrimp, scallops, marinated chicken or all three in a delicious roasted garlic pesto cream sauce tossed with penne pasta.

Circa 1922
8 N. Front St. 762-1922

This charming 1920s decor restaurant offers a tapas-style menu, featuring smaller portions of specialties from around the world. Their extensive array of wines by the glass allows guests to pair their wine with their meal, in an atmosphere that is historic and inviting.

Filet Mignon in Porto Pastry: Topped with gruyere cheese and prosciutto ham, wrapped in puff pastry and served atop a tawny port wine sauce.

Circa's Grilled Pork Tenderloin: Marinated in molasses and served with an apple bourbon sauce and toasted sweet potato bread.

Elijah's
S. Water St. 343-1448

Dine with a panoramic vista of the beautiful Cape Fear River. Our restaurant is an American seafood grill, featuring the Oyster Bar with outdoor dining on the river. Beef, poultry and pasta complement the seafood menu. Be sure to try our Famous Stuff! Lunch and dinner from 11:30 a.m. In Chandler's Wharf.

Carolina Bucket: Steamed clams, crab legs, oysters, mussels, shrimp, sausage, new potatoes, corn on the cob.

Hot Crab Dip: Fresh backfin crabmeat baked in cream, horseradish and cheese, served with garlic croutons.

The Fish Market
6826 Market St. 792-1447

We're not a restaurant, but we supply fresh seafood to many of Wilmington's and Wrightsville Beach's finest restaurants. Let us supply you with the ingredients for your own unforgettable seafood feast, at affordable prices. Also spices, condiments and sauces.

"unbelievable"
Golf Magazine

"Make it a point to visit Sticky Fingers."
Chattanooga Free Press

"delicious"
Food & Wine Magazine

Also Recommended By:
The Atlanta Constitution, Bon Apetit Magazine, The Boston Herald, The Charlotte Observer, The Wall Street Journal & The Today Show

Sticky Fingers
Restaurant and Bar

Wilmington
5044 Market Street
(at the corner of Market & New Centre Drive)
452-RIBS (7427)

stickyfingersONLINE.com

CAFÉ DE FRANCE

French Bistro
Authentic French regional cooking
Outdoor patio with live music

The Forum
1121 Military Cutoff Road
910.256.6600
www.cafedefrance.net

---

36 www.wilmingtontoday.com

Our friendly, expert staff will give you menu advice and cooking tips.

Local shrimp: Fresh off the boat, never frozen. Boiled, steamed, sauteed or deep-fried, you'll taste the difference.

Fresh fish of the day: Snapper, grouper, pompano, mackerel, tuna: space doesn't permit listing all the possibilities.

Grouper Nancy's

501 Nutt St. 251-8009

In an old railroad warehouse on the Cape Fear River, Grouper Nancy's specializes in fresh seafood, steaks, beef, veal, chicken & pasta. Seasonal outdoor dining on deck overlooking the river. Convenient to downtown with free parking. Dinner Tuesday through Saturday.

Grouper Nancy: Fresh grouper fillet sauteed with shrimp, scallions, tomatoes, black olives, green peppercorns, fresh herbs and lemon *beurre blanc* sauce, over angel hair pasta.

Mark's Infamous Crabmeat Stuffed Filet Mignon: Laced with backfin crabmeat grilled to perfection nappered with peppercorn blue cheese sauce, with vegetable and baked potato.

Heck of a Peck

4039 Masonboro Loop Rd. 793-2300

A classic oyster bar serving up the finest oysters, shrimp, clams and scallops. All the flavor and fun of a Carolina oyster roast, without the hassle. An assortment of sides, dipping sauces, beers and wines round out the meal. Midway between Wrightsville & Carolina beaches.

Oysters: in the shell, by the peck or half peck, steamed to order (rare, medium or well done) and shucked for you.

Shrimp: steamed and peeled, mild or spicy, served with cocktail sauce or melted butter.

Henrietta III

101 S. Water St. 343-1611

This antebellum style river boat offers relaxing dinner cruises along the Cape Fear River on Friday and Saturday evenings. The Henrietta features a spacious climate-controlled dining salon, dance floor, entertainment and all ABC permits. Pre-paid reservations required for dinner cruises. Board half-hour prior to departure from Water and Dock streets.

Dinner Buffet: Mixed salad with cherry tomatoes, cucumbers, croutons and house dressing, bakery rolls, lightly seasoned baked chicken, roast beef in gravy, herbed rice, two vegetables in season, two desserts, coffee & tea.

Olympia

212 Causeway Drive. 256-5514

Olympia brings a mediterranean flair to lunches and dinners at Wrightsville

Continued on next page

OLYMPIA
Mediterranean Cuisine
"Food of the Gods"

Fresh Seafood • Crab Legs & Live Lobsters
Steaks & Lamb Chops
Pasta & Salads
Full Bar

Family Dining with Large Selection of Fine Wines and Beer

Open for Dinner 4 p.m.
Sunday 11:30 a.m. - 10:30 p.m.
212 Causeway Drive, Wrightsville Beach

256-5514

GROUPER NANCY'S
FINE DINING & SPIRITS

Casual Fine Dining in a unique location in Wilmington's History

501 Nutt St.,
Coast Line Center
Downtown Wilmington
Open Tuesday - Saturday,
5:30 pm until
All ABC Permits

251-8009

Catering Available

www.wilmingtontoday.com

Dining Guide
Continued from previous page.

Beach. Greek specialties, appetizers and lavish seafood entrees highlight a menu. With famous Greek salads, fine wines and beer. Food of the gods!

Shrimp *a la* Greca: Sauteed shrimp with fresh diced tomatoes, fresh garlic with feta cheese and thyme served over your favorite pasta, with fresh parsley.

Grouper Mykonos: Fresh grilled local grouper filet, with sweet red onion sauce and feta cheese. Served with roasted potatoes.

The Pilot House
S. Water St. 343-0200

In the historic Craig House in Chandler's Wharf, our Cape Fear Riverfront restaurant has served the finest in Southern fare for 25 years. Relax at lunch or dinner in the casual elegance of the dining room, or enjoy a meal on our expansive waterfront deck. Innovative regional sefoods are sure to please the palate. Delicious dishes of beef, fowl, pasta and game. Reservations accepted seven days a week.

Shrimp and Grits: Shrimp, kielbasa sausage, mushrooms, scallions, low country seasoning and fried grits cake.

Sweet Potato Grouper: Baked grouper, greens, mushroom ravioli, fried sweet potato crisps, balsamic vinaigrette.

Sticky Fingers
5044 Market St. 452-7427

Famous for some of the South's best ribs, chicken and barbecue. Founded in Charleston, S.C. in 1992 by three friends who met in high school. Legendary for customer service, it has been praised in many publications.

Carolina Sweet Ribs: The house specialty, tender pork ribs basted with Carolina Sweet Sauce made with real honey. Nothing could be finer!

BBQ Pork Sandwich: Lean, tender BBQ pork piled high on a toasted bun, with our famous barbecue sauce.

Tomatoz
1201 S. College Road. 313-0541

Well-known for its original menu, colorful food and atmosphere, Tomatoz blends Californian, Italian, Mexican and Southern. Sauces, desserts and breads are homemade. Lunch & dinner daily; Sunday brunch and children's menu. Large selection of import and micro brews and wines. All ABC permits.

Garlic Shrimp: Garlic, olive oil, tomatoes, spinach, white wine and lemon over fettucine.

Salmon Veracruz: Olives, capers, tomatoes, jalapenos, black beans, rice and stuffed chili.

Recreation
SPORTS & OUTDOORS

Piney woods to salt marshes and seaside vistas: gorgeous settings make this a golfer's paradise

Chief venues for team sports are on the UNCW campus and at Legion Stadium.

Running, cycling and tennis are all 12-month sports in the Cape Fear area

Fans of team sports can find a variety of games for family entertainment.

Wilmington has NCAA Division I basketball, college baseball, professional soccer and semi-pro football teams.

The venues for these games are on the UNC-Wilmington campus on South College Road and the Legion Stadium sports complex on Carolina Beach Road.

WILMINGTON SHARKS
College summer league baseball

The Wilmington Sharks are part of the Coastal Plain League. They play at Buck Hardee Field in the Legion Stadium athletic complex on Carolina Beach Road. The season is June through August. Tickets cost $4 to $5. 343-5621.

UNCW SEAHAWKS
NCAA basketball

The Seahawks of the University of North Carolina at Wilmington compete in the Colonial Athletic Association. The 2002-03 men's team led by Coach Brad Brownell won the CAA championships and earned an NCAA Tournament bid for the third time in four years. Men's and women's teams play in Trask Coliseum on the UNCW campus. The regular season runs November through February. Tickets: Men's team, $12 adults, $7 children 14 and under; Women's team: $4 adults, children 14 and under free.

NCAA baseball

The Seahawks' baseball season runs from February through May. Home games are played at Brooks Field on the UNCW campus on South College Road. Admission is $4 for adults, free for children 14 and younger.

HAMMERHEADS
Minor league soccer

The Wilmington Hammerheads are part of the USL Pro Select League and affiliated with the Miami Fusion. They play 12 home games this year at Legion Stadium on Carolina Beach Road. The 2003 season opener is March 29; the last game is Aug. 2. Adult tickets cost $8 to $10, children $6 to $8. 796-0076.

PORT CITY DIESEL
Semi-pro football

This start-up team will play a July-September schedule at Legion Stadium. It is part of the Mason Dixon Football League, which includes 20 teams in the Mid-Atlantic states. The 2003 home opener is July19.

Tickets are $7 for adults, $6 students, free for children under 12. 259-3210

UNCW
The Seahawks are 2002 & 2003 CAA champions.

CAPE FEAR COAST CONVENTION & VISITORS BUREAU
Hammerheads soccer team and Sharks baseball team play at Legion sports complex.

www.wilmingtontoday.com

Greenfield Park offers five miles of paved trail and wooden bridges for cycling, running and strolling.

RUNNING & RIDING

With year-round mild climate, Wilmington is a paradise for runners and cyclists. But with congested highways and a scarcity of sidewalks and bike paths, it can take some doing to find good routes.

Here are some favorite places for fitness fans.

The Loop, Wrightsville Beach.
This two-plus-mile circuit follows sidewalks around Wrightsville Beach Park, across Banks Channel and along North Lumina Avenue. It offers fine views of salt marshes and waterways. (Bicycles aren't allowed on the sidewalk.) Parking is available at the town park off Causeway Drive (U.S. 76) and at the Wrightsville Beach Museum off Channel Drive (U.S. 74.)

Greenfield Park, Wilmington.
A five-mile paved path goes around scenic Greenfield Lake, which is lined by towering cypress and pine trees and an abundance of flowering shrubs. Bikes can be rented at the park's concession stand for $5 an hour. Parking is available at the park entrance on South Fifth Avenue and Willard Street, and at several lots around Lake Shore Drive.

Forest Hills loop, Wilmington.
Popular for runners in the area of the YMCA on Market Street, this circuit follows sidewalks on Market Street, Colonial Drive, Wrightsville Avenue and Forest Hills Drive.

River-to-the-Sea bike trail, Wilmington to Wrightsville Beach.
This marked route mostly follows local streets. It starts downtown at Orange Street and meanders southeast to Colwell Avenue. A short stretch of dedicated bike path links riders to Park Avenue, which is the trail's main route toward the ocean. A good base for exploring the trail is Empie Park on Park Avenue near Independence Boulevard, which has abundant free parking.

Eastwood Road, Wilmington.
The most direct route from the Market Street hotel area to Wrightsville Beach, this main highway has a new sidewalk along its north side. Unfortunately, there is a

On The Loop at Wrightsville Beach.

gap with no sidewalks between the Market Street-College Road interchange and the Eastwood sidewalk. Just east of the interchange, use Old Eastwood Road, which connects to Racine Drive, as a safer shortcut to Eastwood. There are also small gaps in the Eastwood sidewalk near the Landfall shopping center. Because of heavy traffic and high speed limits, we recommend against riding in the Eastwood Road vehicle lanes.

River Road bike route, Wilmington to Carolina Beach.
This 12-mile route follows the Cape Fear River between Shipyard Boulevard in Wilmington and the Snows Cut bridge, which leads to Carolina Beach. Paved bike lanes on both sides of River Road are scheduled for construction during 2002.

Pleasure Island bike route, Carolina Beach to Fort Fisher.
Marked bike lanes follow U.S. 421 from the Snows Cut bridge through Carolina Beach and Kure Beach to the Fort Fisher ferry landing.

TENNIS

Tennis is a 12-month sport in our region, with convenient public courts in many areas and active competitive leagues.

Some popular options are:

Empie Park: This city park is Wilmington's leading tennis site. Courts are lighted. Park Avenue at Independence Boulevard. Courts must be reserved at least 24 hours in advance. $4 for 90 minutes. 343-3681 or 343-3682.

Greenfield Park: South Fifth Avenue at Willard Street, off South Third Street (U.S. 421 south.)

Legion Stadium: Lighted courts. Carolina Beach Road (U.S. 421 south.)

A morning tennis lesson at Empie Park's courts.

Hugh MacRae Park: Has lighted courts. South College Road (N.C. 132 south) near Oleander Drive.

Ogden Park: Lighted courts. Entrances from Gordon Road and Market Street (U.S. 17.)

Several other neighborhood parks operated by the City of Wilmington and New Hanover County have public courts, some of them lighted.

Wrightsville Beach: Town park, Causeway Drive (U.S. 76.)

Carolina Beach: Chappel Park at Dow Road and Clarendon Avenue.

Southport: Lowe-White Memorial Park, Leonard and Willis Drive; and Smithfield Park on N.C. 133.

Oak Island: Middleton Park, 47th Street and Oak Island Drive.

Also, many hotels and resorts have private courts for their guests' use.

Golf
YEAR-ROUND SPORT

Golf has a long tradition here, starting with the Cape Fear Country Club in 1896.

Wilmington's 'Muni' course was designed in the 1920s by Donald Ross

PGA greats have put their signatures on many of the region's new courses.

Golf packages offered by hotels and travel agencies make it easy to experience the region's best courses.

Gorgeous settings, ranging from piney woods to salt marsh and seaside vistas, combine with mild climate to make the Cape Fear Coast a golfer's paradise.

That's why Golf Digest magazine ranked Wilmington No. 8 in its "Best Little Golf Towns" survey in November 2002. The magazine rated a place's "golfability" by such factors as courses per capita, cost and quality of courses, and weather.

The top-ranked places tended to be moderate-sized towns "with a good selection of medium-price three- and four-star courses."

Not as widely recognized as such nearby golf destinations as the Sandhills or Myrtle Beach, our region's courses tend to be less crowded and more affordable.

Golf has a long tradition here, starting with the Cape Fear Country Club in 1896. The city-owned Wilmington Golf Course (known as "Muni") was developed in the 1920s. Laid out by the legendary designer Donald Ross, the course was restored to its original form in the 1990s.

Most of the newer courses that have sprung up along the coast are part of residential real estate developments. Some of these have become full-fledged towns. All lure home buyers with fairway views and year-round play. These golf communities are found in the Topsail area, in Wilmington and near Carolina Beach. But the greatest concentration is in Brunswick County, which boasts great beaches and easy drives to both Wilmington and Myrtle Beach.

Golf packages offered by area hotels and travel agencies make it easy for visiting players to experience some of the region's best courses.

SEE: Weather and climate on page 31.

MAGNOLIA GREENS
Soaring trees and challenging water hazards abound at Brunswick County's many courses. Here, Magnolia Greens' 18th hole.

DRIVING RANGES

Wilmington has two commercial driving ranges not affiliated with courses. The Valley center was for sale in early 2003.

Coastal Golf Center: 6987 Market St. 791-9010

Valley Golf Center & Driving Range: 4416 S. College Road. 395-2750

CAPE FEAR COAST CONVENTION & VISITORS BUREAU
Green at The Cape, near Carolina Beach.

Courses
Yardage, par, ratings

BALD HEAD ISLAND
PO Box 3070, Bald Head Island 28461.
457-7310, (800) 234-1666. Access by ferry.
Designer: George Cobb **18 holes, par 72.**

	Blue	White	Gold	Red
Yardage	6855	6239	5536	4862
Slope	139	126	117	117
Rating	74.3	71.6	68.6	70.1

Green fees: $74-$119, incl. cart and ferry. Carts required during peak season
Credit cards: V, MC, AE, D

BEAU RIVAGE PLANTATION
649 Rivage Promenade, Wilmington 28412
392-9022 Off U.S. 421 south.
Designer: Joe Getsner **18 Holes, par 72**

	Blue	White	Red	Black
Yardage	6166	5610	4612	6709
Slope	129	126	114	136
Rating	69.9	67.8	67.1	72.4

Green fees: $25 to $40. Carts required.
Credit cards: V, MC, AE, D

BELVEDERE PLANTATION
2368 Country Club Drive, Hampstead 28443
270-2703 Off U.S. 17 north.
Designer: Russell Burney **18 holes, par 71**

	Blue	Gold	Green	Black
Yardage	5824	5171	4539	6350
Slope	128	118	116	131
Rating	71.0	67.3	69.2	72.3

Green fees: $20 to $25. Carts required.
Credit cards: V, MC

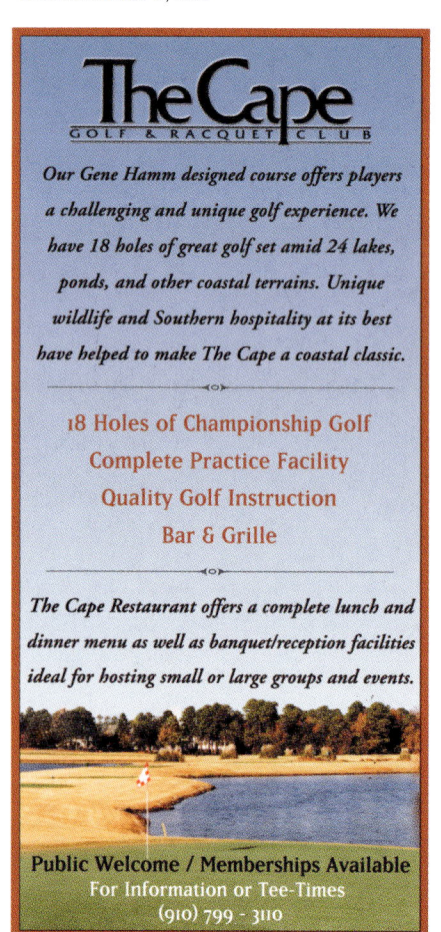

The Cape
GOLF & RACQUET CLUB

Our Gene Hamm designed course offers players a challenging and unique golf experience. We have 18 holes of great golf set amid 24 lakes, ponds, and other coastal terrains. Unique wildlife and Southern hospitality at its best have helped to make The Cape a coastal classic.

18 Holes of Championship Golf
Complete Practice Facility
Quality Golf Instruction
Bar & Grille

The Cape Restaurant offers a complete lunch and dinner menu as well as banquet/reception facilities ideal for hosting small or large groups and events.

Public Welcome / Memberships Available
For Information or Tee-Times
(910) 799 - 3110

THE CAPE
535 The Cape Blvd. Wilmington 28412
791-9292 Off U.S. 421 south.
Designer: Gene Hamm **18 Holes, Par 72**

	Blue	White	Gold	Green
Yardage	6805	6129	5629	4948
Slope	133	125	120	118
Rating	73.1	69.9	67.5	69.3

Green Fees: $35-$45. Carts required.
Credit Cards: V,MC

CAROLINA NATIONAL
1643 Goley Hewett Rd. SE, Bolivia 28422
755-5200; (888) 200-6455
Designers: Fred Couples and Gene Bates
27 holes, par 72

	Blue	White	Black	Teal
Yardage	6000	4760	7000	5400
Slope	143	132	136	120
Rating	72.1	69.2	73.4	66.3

Green fees: $55 to $95. Carts required.
Credit cards: V, MC, AE, DS

CASTLE BAY
2516 Hoover Road, Hampstead 28443
270-1978 Off U.S. 17 north.
Designer: Randy Blanton **18 Holes, Par 72**

	Gold	Blue	White	Green	Red
Yardage	6713	6328	5793	5466	4717
Slope	140	134	123	118	121
Rating	72.3	70.8	69.0	67.4	67.9

Green Fees: $50-29 incl. cart, required.
Credit Cards: V, MC AMEX DIS

DUCK HAVEN
1202 Eastwood Rd., Wilmington 28403
791-7983, 313-0795
18 holes, par 72

	Blue	White	Red
Yardage	6500	6000	5360
Slope	125	122	N/A
Rating	71.6	69.7	N/A

Green fees: $13 to $25 incl. cart, not required.
Credit Cards: Not accepted

ECHO FARMS
4114 Echo Farms Blvd., Wilmington 28412
791-9318, 799-0324
Designers: Gene Hamm, Ian Scott
18 holes, par 72

	Blue	White	Red	Gold
Yardage	6611	5904	5043	7095
Slope	123	123	114	136
Rating	71.3	71.3	72.3	74.6

Green fees: $25 to $35
Hours: 7 a.m.-6 p.m. off season; 7 a.m.-7 p.m. during season. Carts required.
Credit cards: V, MC, AE, D

FOUNDERS CLUB
at St. James Plantation
3021 Beaver Creek Drive, Southport 28461
253-9500, (800) 247-4806
Designer: P.B. Dye **18 holes, par 72**

	Gold	Black	White	Green	Red
Yardage	7004	6413	5852	5390	5040
Slope	151	143	137	130	131
Rating	76.2	73.0	70.6	68.5	70.5

Green fees: $45. Carts required.
Credit cards: V, MC

CAPE FEAR MUSEUM

This 1901 photo shows Cape Fear Country Club, Wilmington's first golf course, founded in 1896.

GREENHILLS
1427 Greenhill Road, Winnabow 28451
253-8333
9 holes, par 35

	Blue	White	Red
Yardage	2389	2212	1953

Green fees: $10 to $13. Carts not required.
Credit cards: V, MC, DS, AE

INLAND GREENS
5945 Inland Greens Drive, Wilmington 28405
452-9900
18 holes, par 54
Yardage: 2001
Green fees: $5 to $8. Carts not required.
Credit cards: not accepted

THE LAKES
591 S. Shore Dr, Boiling Spring Lakes 28461.
845-2625
Designer: Ed Riciboni **18 holes, par 72**

	Blue	White	Red
Yardage	6760	6208	5349
Slope	131	125	124
Rating	72.7	70.3	70.6

Green fees: $21 to $30. Carts not required.
Credit cards: V, MC

LOCKWOOD FOLLY
19 Clubhouse Drive SW, Holden Beach 28462
842-5666, (877) 562-9663
Designer: Willard Byrd **18 holes, par**

	Blue	White	Red	Gold
Yardage	6836	6167	5029	5524
Slope	139	128	122	121
Rating	73.8	70.8	70.9	67.8

Green fees: $35 to $70. Carts required.
Credit cards: V, MC

WEST BRUNSWICK COURSES
For details about the many golf courses in western Brunswick County, including Ocean Isle Beach, Shallotte, Sunset Beach and Calabash, see our online golf directory at **www.wilmingtontoday.com**

Or search our online golf database for area or amenities.

Good weather for golfing comes
in all 12 months of the year.

A winter day at Wilmington Golf Course, best known as 'Muni.'
JOHN MEYER

MAGNOLIA GREENS
1800 Linkwood Circle, Leland 28451.
383-0999; (800) 677-7524 Off U.S. 17 south.
Designer: Tom Jackson **27 holes, par 72**

	Black	Blue	White	Red
Yardage	7156	6619	5936	5173
Slope	138	130	119	120
Rating	75.3	72	68.6	70.3

Green fees: $29 to $59 + $15 cart, required.
Credit cards: V, MC, AE, DS

MEMBERS CLUB
at St. James Plantation
3779 Members Club Blvd., Southport 28461
253-9500; (800) 474-9277 Off N.C. 211.
Designer: Hale Irwin **27 holes, par 72**

	Gold	Black	White	Teal
Yardage	6887	6447	5948	5113
Slope	135	124	119	123
Rating	73.9	71.4	69.2	71.0

Green fees: $40 to $100 Carts required.
Credit cards: V, MC

NORTH SHORE
N.C. Hwy. 210, North Topsail Beach 28460
327-2410; (800) 828-5035
Designer: Bob Moore **18 holes, par 72**

	Blue	White	Red	Gold
Yardage	6866	6358	5039	5636
Slope	134	123	122	119
Rating	72.8	70.8	68.7	67.3

Green fees: $28 to $55. Carts required before 3 p.m.
Credit cards: V, MC

OAK ISLAND
928 Caswell Beach Rd., Oak Island 28465
278-5275; (800) 278-5275
Designer: George Cobb **18 holes, par 72**

	Blue	White	Red	Black
Yardage	6608	5934	5428	6135
Slope	128	122	121	124
Rating	71.8	69.6	71.4	70.1

Green fees: $30 to $55. Carts required.
Credit cards: V, MC

OLDE POINT
P.O. Box 249, Hampstead 28443
270-2403 or 270-4554 Off U.S. 17 north
18 holes, par 72

	Blue	White	Red	Gold
Yardage	6913	6008	5133	6253
Slope	130	120	118	123
Rating	73.1	69.3	69.8	70.4

Green fees: $26 to $45. Carts required.
Credit cards: V, MC

OLD FORT
N.C. Hwy 133 South, Winnabow 28479
371-9940
18 holes, par 72

	Blue	White	Red
Yardage	6311	5575	4588
Slope	108	103	99
Rating	68.4	65.9	64.6

Green fees: $15 to $20. Carts not required.
Credit cards: Not accepted

PLAYERS CLUB
at St. James Plantation)
3640 Players Club Drive, Southport 28461
457-0049; (800) 281-6626 Off N.C. 211.
Designer: Tim Cate **18 holes, par 72**

	Gold	Black	White	Green	Teal
Yardage	6940	6402	6000	5447	4907
Slope	150	142	134	122	121
Rating	74.6	71.7	70.1	67.4	69.6

Green fees: $45 to $99. Carts required.
Credit cards: V, MC

PORTER'S NECK PLANTATION
8403 Vintage Club Circle, Wilmington 28411
686-1177 Off U.S. 17 to Porters Neck Road.
Designer: Tom Fazio **18 holes, par 72**

	Blue	White	Red	Gold	Green
Yardage	6686	6205	5145	7112	5655
Slope	132	128	121	136	125
Rating	72.8	70.4	70.5	75.3	68.3

Green fees: $40 to $75 Carts not required.
Credit cards: V, MC

RIVER LANDING
116 Paddle Wheel Drive, Wallace 28466
285-6693; (800) 959-3056 Off I-40.
Designer: Clyde Johnston **27 holes, par 72**

	Blue	White	Red	Gold	Yellow
Yardage	6590	6074	4870	7009	5737
Slope	130	121	116	138	116
Rating	71.4	69.0	69.0	73.6	67.9

Green fees: $59 to $69 incl. cart, not required.
Credit cards: V, MC, AE

TOPSAIL GREENS
U.S. Hwy 17 North, Hampstead, 28445
270-2883
Designer: Russell Burney **18 holes, par 71**

	Blue	White	Red
Yardage	6324	6010	5033
Slope	121	118	113
Rating	70.8	68.8	68.8

Green Fees: $30-35. Carts required.
Credit Cards: MC, V

ST. JAMES PLANTATION
SEE: Founders, Members, Players clubs.

WILMINGTON MUNICIPAL
311 S. Wallace Ave., Wilmington 28409
791-0558 Off Oleander Drive.
Designer: Donald Ross **18 holes, par 71**

	Blue	White	Red
Yardage	6550	6300	5500
Slope	128	123	119
Rating	71.8	70.6	69

Green fees: $16-$17 + $10 cart, not required.
Credit cards: V, MC

Magnolia Greens
GOLF PLANTATION
Rated ★★★★ By Golf Digest
Host of 1998 & 1999 PGA Tour Qualifying

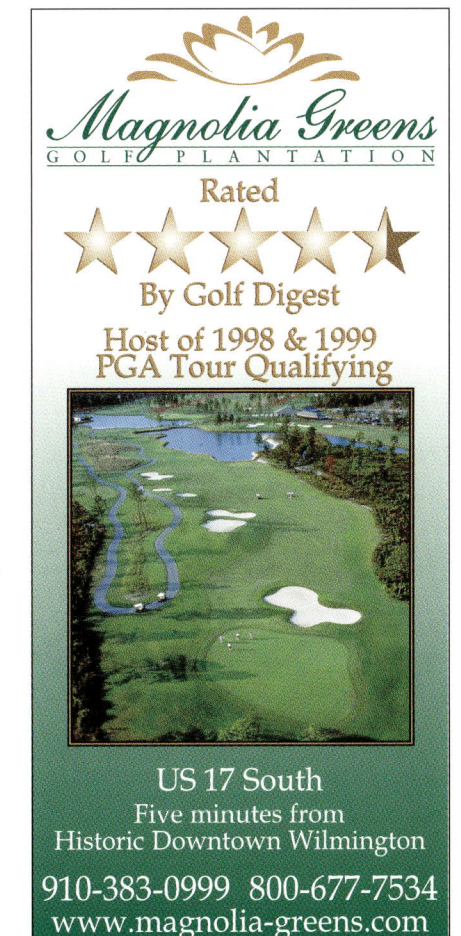

US 17 South
Five minutes from
Historic Downtown Wilmington
910-383-0999 800-677-7534
www.magnolia-greens.com

www.wilmingtontoday.com

Panoramic view from downtown waterfront shows 1. Cape Fear Memorial Bridge (U.S. 17-74-76); 2. State Port; 3. Military rapid response ships and tugboats; 4. Eagles Island ; 5. River taxi dock; 6. Battleship North Carolina; 7. Cape Fear River and U.S. 421 bridge; 8. Point Peter; 9. Northeast Cape Fear River; and 10. Sutton power plant.

On the water
River vistas and boating fun

What's that ship? Scenes from a Wilmington harbor cruise

JOHN MEYER

Coast Guard cutter 'Diligence' seen from across river.

JOHN MEYER

As container ships unload at State Port, workers make repairs on barge beached on Eagles Island shoreline.

Wilmington began as a seaport, and it remains North Carolina's largest port. Commercial wharves once lined downtown's waterfront, as well as the opposite shore on Eagles Island. But most ships now dock at the State Port down river from the Cape Fear Memorial Bridge.

Bulk freighters and tankers still pass through the vertical-lift drawbridge on their way to terminals on the Northeast Cape Fear River upstream.

The photos on this page may help visitors interpret what they see from Wilmington's waterfront and bridges.

Daytime and evening river cruises can provide an up-close look at these scenes and others up and down the river.

Take a ferry ride across the Cape Fear. SEE page 24.

Tips for boaters

Alcohol: State law sets the same standard for boat operators as for drivers: a maximum blood alcohol level of .08 percent. Wildlife officers and sheriff's deputies patrol waterways and enforce boating regulations.

Water scooters: Personal watercraft operators must be at least 16, or 13 if they have a valid boater safety certificate. Speeds are limited to 5 mph in marshes, near piers, shores, swimmers or surf fishermen.

DICK PARROTT

'Cape Johnson' and 'Cape Juby' are called on as needed to carry Army equipment on overseas deployments.

DICK PARROTT

Tugboat fleet guides ocean-going ships along the Cape Fear River channel and into Wilmington's harbor.

DICK PARROTT

Barge and towboat is a common scene on the river.

DICK PARROTT

Rotting hulks and rusting machinery are remains of tugboats abandoned in the 1930s on the Eagles Island shoreline.

44 www.wilmingtontoday.com

Public boat ramps

Ownership/management code:

US = U.S. Army Corps of Engineers
NCP = N.C. State Park.
NCW = N.C. Wildlife Resources Commission.
Local = City, town or county.

Intracoastal Waterway

North Topsail Beach: From N.C. 210 eastbound, turn left immediately after crossing Intracoastal Waterway bridge to ramp. *NCW.*

Wrightsville Beach: From U.S. 74-76 eastbound, turn right immediately after crossing drawbridge. Follow roadway under bridge to ramp. Provides access to ocean through Masonboro Inlet: south on waterway to marker 129, then left; or through Banks Channel. *NCW.*

Carolina Beach/Snows Cut: From U.S. 421 southbound, turn right immediately after crossing Snows Cut bridge; follow roadway under bridge to ramp at east end of Snows Cut. Provides access to ocean through Carolina Beach Inlet: north on waterway to marker 155A; and to Cape Fear River, west through Snows Cut. *NCW.*

Oak Island: From N.C. 133 southbound, turn left just before Oak Island bridge on Fish Factory Road. Follow road one-half mile to ramp. *NCW.*

Sunset Harbor: From Southport or Oak Island, follow N.C. 211 westbound. Turn left (south) on Sunset Harbor Road. Follow road six miles to ramp. *NCW.*

Holden Beach: From N.C. 130 southbound, cross Holden Beach bridge, turn left on Ocean Boulevard. Turn left again on Jordan Street to ramp under bridge. *NCW.*

Cape Fear River

Fort Fisher: From Kure Beach, follow U.S. 421 to end near ferry landing. Provides access to "The Basin" and The Rocks-Zeke Island area for shallow-draft boats. No direct access to the river. *NCW.*

Carolina Beach State Park: From N.C. 421 southbound, turn right on Dow Road immediately after crossing Snows Cut Bridge. From Dow Road, turn right on State Park Road into park. Follow signs to marina. Access to Snows Cut, which connects to river and Intracoastal Waterway. *NCP.*

Wilmington: Dram Tree Park. From South Front Street, turn west on Castle Street. Ramp is at end of street. *Local.*

Kings Bluff (Lock & Dam #1): Off N.C. 87 west of Riegelwood. North on Kings Bluff Road to river. Ramp is below dam. *US.*

Elwell Ferry: Off N.C. 87 east of Elizabethtown. North on Elwell Ferry Road to river. *NCW.*

Brown's Landing (Lock & Dam #2): From N.C. 87 east of Elizabethtown, turn right on N.C 87 business. Turn right at bottom of hill, follow road ½ mile north to ramp. Ramp is below dam. *US.*

Tory Hole: U.S. 701 north of N.C. 87 business in Elizabethtown. Turn left just before bridge; ramp is under bridge. *NCW.*

Brunswick River

Belville: From U.S. 17-74-76, take N.C. 133 southbound. Ramp is on Belville Town Park, on left (east) side of highway. *Local.*

Black River

Hunts Bluff: West of Currie and Moore's Creek battlefield. Follow N.C. 210 west, turn right on Morgan Road, right on Hunt's Bluff Road (gravel) to river. *NCW.*

Northeast Cape Fear River

Castle Hayne: From U.S. 117 northbound, turn right on Orange Street just past Castle Hayne business district, just before bridge. *NCW.*

Holly Shelter: From I-40, follow N.C. 210 eastbound, cross Northeast Cape Fear River Bridge; immediately after bridge, turn left (north) on Shaw Highway. Follow Shaw Highway about six miles to ramp. *NCW.*

Lake Waccamaw

Town of Lake Waccamaw: From U.S. 74-76 westbound, turn left at Lake Waccamaw intersection. Turn right (west) on N.C. 214 to Flemington Drive. Turn left to Lake Shore Drive. Bear right on Lake Shore Drive and 2.4 mi to ramp. *NCW.*

Lake Waccamaw park: From Flemington Drive, turn left on Bella Coola Road, following state park signs. Ramp is just outside state park. *Local.*

Waccamaw River

Pireway: From Sunset Beach, follow N.C. 904 northbound 10 miles. Ramp is on right at bridge. *NCW.*

Other waters

Sutton Lake (north of Wilmington): From Wilmington, follow U.S. 421 northbound about three miles. Turn left (west) on Sutton Lake Road to ramp. *NCW*

Rice's Creek (south of Leland): From U.S. 17 southbound, turn left (east) on Governor's Road. *NCW*

SEE: Map on page 24.
SEE: Fishing on page 46 and 47.

Many private marinas offer in-water mooring; some also have dry-stack storage. Transient docking is available along city's Riverwalk, Downtown.

DICK PARROTT

www.wilmingtontoday.com

Fishing
Ocean, sound, freshwater

Fighting big deep-sea gamefish. Surf-casting for blues. Exploring a quiet stream in a bass boat. Whatever the flavor, fishing is a favorite local pastime.

The easiest approaches to salt water are in the surf and on ocean piers. Bait and tackle shops can provide advice on what's biting and the best gear.

For trips offshore or to the Gulf Stream, charter boats are available for hire at Carolina Beach, Southport, Wrightsville Beach, Topsail Beach and other towns. Scheduled head boats from Carolina Beach will take anglers for a day's fishing and provide all tackle.

Fishing Piers
Call for hours and rates.

Wrightsville Beach:
Johnnie Mercer's, 23 E. Salisbury St. 256-4469

Carolina & Kure beaches:
Carolina Beach, North End. 458-5518
Kure Beach Pier, Avenue K. 458-5524

Topsail Island:
Seaview, N. Topsail Beach. 328-3171
Ocean City, Surf City. 328-5701
Surf City Ocean, 114 S Shore Dr, 328-3521
Jolly Roger, 803 Ocean Blvd. 633-3196

Oak Island:
Yaupon Beach, 705 Ocean Dr. 278-9400
Ocean Crest, 1411 E Beach Dr. 278-3333
Long Beach, 2729 W Beach Dr. 278-5962

Tackle & Technique

These tips on what to catch and how come from Tex's Tackle.

The Gulf Stream (50+ miles) is home to "bluewater" fish: yellow fin tuna, white and blue marlin, sailfish and wahoo. March-May and October-November are prime seasons. Baits include rigged ballyhoo and lures trolled at 5 to 9 knots. You could hook a 5 pound mahi-mahi or a 500 pound blue marlin!

Offshore waters (3 to 50 miles) offer a huge variety of species: king mackerel, amberjack and cobia. Kings are caught by slow trolling (1 to 1.5 knots) live bait. Other species are caught while targeting kings. Cobia, amberjack, and mahi mahi frequently will light your reel up. Expect good bottom-fishing action almost any time, but spring and fall tend to be best. Grouper, sea bass and snapper will hit a variety of fresh or frozen baits. Check with your local tackle shop for current catch limits and size restrictions.

SUNDOWN CHARTERS

- Fishing
- Tournaments
- Cruises
- Beach outings

Experience an unforgettable day on the water in our 25-foot Trophy with Cuddy Cabin

Captain Mike LaVeine   793-6262 Cell: 612-5162
USCG #961541

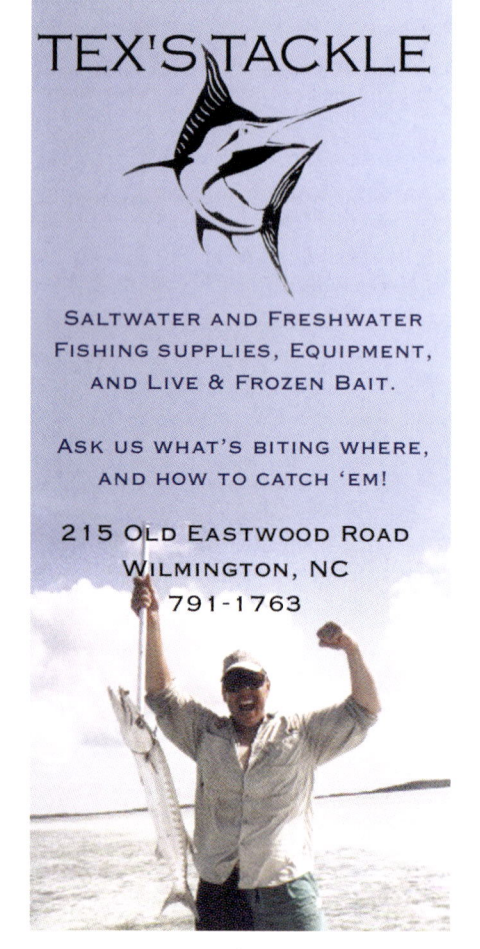

TEX'S TACKLE

Saltwater and Freshwater Fishing Supplies, Equipment, and Live & Frozen Bait.

Ask us what's biting where, and how to catch 'em!

215 Old Eastwood Road
Wilmington, NC
791-1763

www.wilmingtontoday.com

Near shore (out to 3 miles) is perfect for the small boater or novice angler. Spanish mackerel and bluefish provide plenty of action, April through October. Although smaller than kings, Spanish more than make up for their size in numbers and tasty flesh. Troll "clark spoons" or similar artificials at about 5 knots just off the beach in 20 to 40 feet of water. The lighter the tackle you use, the more fun these fish are.

Surf and pier fishing is productive March through November, but fall is best for variety and larger fish. In spring, look for bluefish, flounder, trout and red drum. Warm summer water brings more species in close. Spanish and king mackerel, cobia, tarpon, and amberjack are routinely caught from piers. Fall brings the annual southern migration of tasty pan-size spots. Bloodworms or fresh shrimp on a two-hook bottom rig will fill your cooler when the run is going on.

CAPE FEAR COAST CONVENTION & VISITORS BUREAU
A great catch is in easy reach via numerous offshore charter fishing boats.

Creeks and sounds: Easily reached by the small boater, flounder, puppy drum, trout, blues and more are caught nearly year round. Live minnows on any typical flounder rig will take blues, trout, flounder and puppy drum. The same bottom rig used on piers works just fine off the boat or bank for spots, croakers and other bottom dwellers.

SEE: Tours & cruises on page 26.
SEE: Boat ramps on page 45.

CONVENTION & VISITORS BUREAU
A king mackerel tournament winner.

FISHING TOURNAMENTS
April 26: Carolina Panfish, Castle Hayne. 763-2453.
May 30-31: Bald Head Island Fishing Rodeo, Bald Head. 457-7500
June 7, Youth Pier Fishing, Kure Beach. 458-2977
June 6-8, Wildlife Bait & Tackle Flounder, Southport, 457-9903
June 6-8, U.S. Open Pier, Oak Island, 457-6964
June 17, Carolina Panfish Free Children's Tournament. 763-2453
June 27-29: Greater Wilmington King Mackerel, Wilmington. 686-4131
June 27-28: Cape Fear Blue Marlin, Wrightsville Beach. 256-6666
July 11-13: East Coast Got-Em-On Classic, Carolina Beach. 458-6729
July 18-20: Long Bay Challenge, Holden Beach. 846--3463.
July 25-26: Capt. Eddy Haneman Sailfish, Wrightsville Beach. 256-6550
July 26: King of the Cape Classic, Southport. 278-4575
Aug. 1-3: Long Bay Lady Anglers King Mackerel, Southport. 278-4137
Aug. 22-24: Topsail Offshore King Mackerel, Topsail Beach. 270-2441
Aug. 29-30: South Brunswick Islands King Mackerel, Holden Beach. 754-6644
Sept. 5-7, Wildlife Bait & Tackle Flounder, Southport, 457-9903
Sept. 18-20: Wrightsville Beach King Mackerel. 799-6483
Oct. 2-4: U.S. Open King Mackerel, Southport. 457-5787
Oct. 4: Captain Charlie's Kid Fishing, Southport. 457-7945
Oct. 3-5: Seagull Bait & Tackle Surf Fishing, Carolina Beach. 458-7135
Oct. 17-18: Fall Brawl Kingfish, Holden Beach. 754-6644

Fortune Hunter Charters
WRIGHTSVILLE BEACH NORTH CAROLINA

31' Bertram Sportfisherman

"Specializing in trolling"
Spanish & King Mackerel, Mahi Mahi, Sailfish, and more...
Full, Three-Quarter and Half-Day Charters

Also offering inshore charters for flounder, trout and more on board the Fortune Hunter Too!

Captain Jimmy Vass • (Mobile) 617-4160   (Office) 791-6414
www.fortunehuntercharters.com

www.wilmingtontoday.com

Hunting
Game lands, regulations

STATE GAME LANDS

The N.C. Wildlife Resources Commission manages these areas for public use. Some limit hunting to Mondays, Wednesdays and Saturdays; others allow hunting six days a week, excluding Sundays. Hunters on state game lands must have a special game land license. To fish on game lands, only a fishing license is needed.

For locations, see map on page 24.

Columbus County black bear sanctuary. 6,022 acres. Along U.S. 74-76 east of Lake Waccamaw. M-W-S.

Holly Shelter game land. 50,120 acres. Northwest of U.S. 17 between Hampstead and Holly Ridge. Access gates off U.S. 17, N.C. 210 and Shaw Highway. Waterfowl impoundments, handicapped hunter access points. M-W-S.

Cape Fear River Wetlands game land. 4,009 acres total. Three tracts: Roan Island, 2,757 acres at Black and Cape Fear rivers, boat access only; two tracts on Northeast Cape Fear River in Pender County. 6 days.

Green Swamp black bear sanctuary. 14,851 acres. East of N.C. 211 north of Supply. M-W-S.

Brunswick County game land. 1,139 acres. East of U.S. 17. Access off Governor's Road SE. 6 days.

Sutton Lake game land. 3,322 acres. West of U.S. 421 along Cape Fear River. Access and boat ramp off Sutton Lake Road. 6 days.

Overgrown farm fields are prime territory for quail. Season is November through February.

N.C. WILDLIFE RESOURCES

LICENSE REQUIREMENTS

No license is required for hook-and-line fishing in salt water. This includes offshore, pier and surf fishing, and fishing in most tidal waters including the Intracoastal Water-way. A state freshwater fishing license is required in waters of the Cape Fear River and its tributaries upstream from downtown Wilmington.

Licenses can be purchased through the Wildlife Resources Commission web site, or from a state license agent. Most sporting goods, tackle and gun shops sell hunting and fishing licenses.

www.ncwildlife.org

HUNTING REGULATIONS

North Carolina's game laws and regulations include many details, exceptions and local rules. Complete regulations can be obtained through state license agents or on the web.

Applies only to the region within 60 miles of Wilmington.

Deer: Either sex. Limit: 2 per day, 6 per season, of which two must be antlerless.
 ♦ Bow only: Sept. 8-Oct. 1.
 ♦ Muzzle-loader only: Oct. 6-12.
 ♦ Gun: Oct. 13-Jan. 1

Bear: Limit 1 per season. Nov. 11-Jan. 1, except Brunswick & Columbus: Dec. 10-Jan. 1

Wild turkey: Bearded turkeys only. Limits: Daily, 1; season, 2. April 13-May 11. No hunting in New Hanover County, part Pender & Columbus.

Quail: Limits: Daily, 6; possession, 12. Nov. 17-Feb. 28.

Grouse: Limits: Daily, 3; possession, 6; season: 30. Oct. 15-Feb. 28.

Migratory birds: Federal regulations take precedence. State seasons and limits for doves and non-migratory Canada geese are announced each year by Aug. 1; for waterfowl by Sept. 1. See web or call (800) 675-0263.

Freshwater fishing: Year-round in all freshwater areas in the Cape Fear Region, except: Sutton Lake closed for small-mouth bass Dec. 1-March 31. See web for limits and size rules.

Saltwater fishing: Regulated by N.C. Division of Marine Fisheries. See web size and catch limits.

www.ncfisheries.net

State License fees	N.C. Resident	Non-res.
Fishing, state-wide, 12 months	$15	$30
Fishing, state-wide, 1 day	$5	$10
Fishing, state-wide, 3 days	N/A	$15
Comp. fishing,[1] 12 months	$20	N/A
Hunting, state-wide, 12 months	$15	$60
Big game privilege,[2] 12 months	$10	$60
Non-resident bear & wild boar	N/A	$125
Hunting, state-wide, 6 days	N/A	$40
Big game privilege,[2] 6 days	N/A	$40
Game lands permit	$15	$15
Waterfowl[3]	$10	$10
Comp. hunting,[4] 12 months	$30	N/A
Sportsman,[5] 12 months	$40	N/A

[1] Comprehensive fishing permits fishing in designated trout waters.

[2] Big game permit required for deer, bear, wild boar and wild turkey. Non-resident big game privilege does not include bear or wild boar. Includes bow hunting and muzzle-loading guns during special seasons.

[3] Federal duck stamp required

[4] Comprehensive hunting includes big game, bow and muzzle-loading hunting, game land permit, waterfowl.

[5] Sportsman is combined comprehensive hunting and fishing license.

Amusements
Fun, games and adventures

This is a sampling of some of the Cape Fear region's commercial attractions and amusement spots.

ALLEIGH'S
Entertainment complex including dinner theater, game room, jazz and blues bar, sports bar and large full-service dining room. Open 11:30 a.m.-1 a.m. daily. 4925 New Center Drive, 793-0999.

AQUATIC SAFARIS
Scuba diving lessons & charters. 5751-4 Oleander Drive. 392-4386.

BLOWING IN THE WIND
Kiteboard lessons & rentals. Cotton Exchange, 312 Nutt St., 763-1730.

BOTTOM TIME
Scuba diving lessons & charters. 6014 Wrightsville Ave., 397-0181.

CARDINAL LANES
Bowling alley, snack bar, arcade games. 7026 Market St., 686-4223; 3907 Shipyard Blvd., 799-3023.

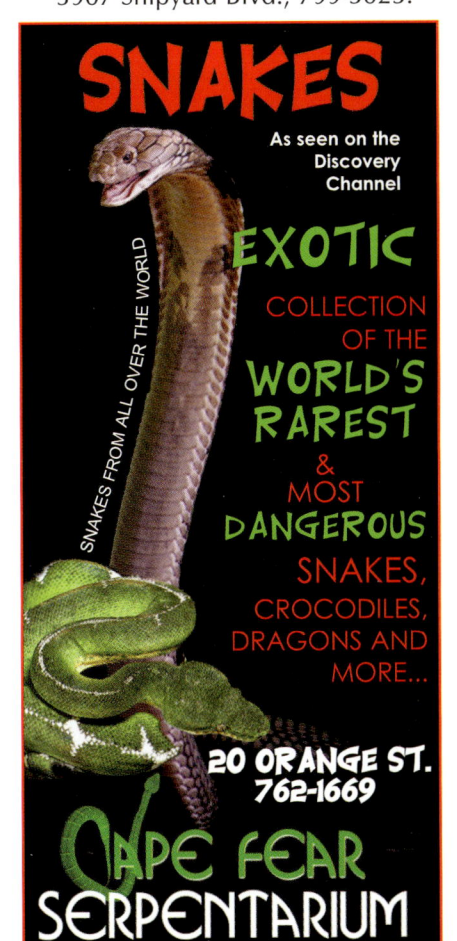

Wilmington isn't big on bright lights and splashy shows. But there are lots of places to have fun.

CAROLINA BEACH JUNGLE GOLF
Miniature golf, batting cages, arcade. 906 Lake Park Blvd. Carolina Beach, 458-8888.

CAROLINA COASTAL ADVENTURES
Kayak, canoe & motorboat tours, nature expeditions. Carolina Beach, 458-9111.

DESPERADO TRAIL RIDES
Horse riding. 7214 N.C. Hwy 210, Rocky Point. 675-0487.

GREENFIELD GRIND SKATE PARK
Public skateboard park. Greenfield Park, South Fifth Avenue at Willard Street. 362-8222.

JELLYBEANS SKATING CENTER
Roller rink and arcade games. 5216 Oleander Drive, 791-6000.

JUBILEE AMUSEMENT PARK
Amusement rides, water slide, race tracks and arcade. 1000 N. Lake Park Blvd., Carolina Beach, 458-9017.

JUNGLE RAPIDS
Waterslide, laser tag, go-cart track, miniature golf and arcade games. 5320 Oleander Drive, 791-0666.

KAYAK CAROLINA
Kayak rentals, lessons and tours. Carolina & Wrightsville beaches, 458-9111.

PUTT PUTT GOLF & GAMES
Miniature golf and arcade games. 4117 Oleander Drive, 392-6660.

SCOOTERS FAMILY SKATING
Skating rink, arcade games. 341 Shipyard Blvd., 791-8550.

THE STADIUM
Baseball and softball batting cages. 5570 Oleander Drive, 791-9660.

TEN PIN ALLEY
Bowling alley, restaurant & lounge. 127 S. College Road, 452-5455.

TOTE-EM-IN ZOO
Small zoo featuring more than 100 animals, reptiles and birds. 5811 Carolina Beach Road, 791-0472.

WATERWAYS SAILING & CHARTERS
Sailing lessons and charters. 2030 Eastwood Road. 256-4282.

For other ideas about things to do, SEE:
- Museums, page 15.
- Historic sites, page 18.
- Tours and cruises, page 26.
- Festivals and events, page 31.
- Sports, page 39.
- Golf, page 41.
- Fishing, page 46.
- Art museums and galleries, page 50.
- Performing arts, page 54.
- Day trips, page 60.

JAY CURLEY
One of 13 cobra varieties.

SERPENTARIUM
The Cape Fear Serpentarium on Orange Street Downtown features one of the world's leading collections of reptiles.

The owner, Dean Ripa, has collected snakes and other exotic reptiles from around the world. These specimens – some of the world's most venomous – are displayed in simulations of their natural habitats. The serpentarium's hundreds of exhibits occupy 6,000 square feet on two floors. Among the exhibits are:
- 15 species of vipers, including bushmasters, the world's largest.
- 13 species of cobra.
- A 23-foot-long, 200-pound reticulated python.
- "Lucy," a giant monitor lizard.

Hours: 11 a.m.-5 p.m., 11-6 Sat., closed Tues. April-October; 11 a.m.-5 p.m., 11-6 Sat., closed Tues-Wed. November-March.

Admission: $7 adults, $6 children 3-15. 20 Orange St. Downtown. 762-1669.

SNAKES
As seen on the Discovery Channel

EXOTIC COLLECTION OF THE WORLD'S RAREST & MOST DANGEROUS SNAKES, CROCODILES, DRAGONS AND MORE...

SNAKES FROM ALL OVER THE WORLD

20 ORANGE ST.
762-1669

CAPE FEAR SERPENTARIUM

www.wilmingtontoday.com

Louise Wells Cameron Art Museum

Wilmington's fine arts centerpiece is the Louise Wells Cameron Art Museum at South 17th Street and Independence Boulevard. In its new building, the museum continues the tradition of the former St. John's Museum.

Founded in 1962, the museum has been dedicated to collecting North Carolina art. Sustained for years by volunteers and a shoestring budget, it has evolved into an important North Carolina cultural institution. A major fund-raising campaign has made the museum into a work of art itself.

The new name honors the late wife of the museum's chief benefactor, businessman Bruce B. Cameron.

The New York architect Charles Gwathmey designed the building. A North Carolina native, his best-known museum project is the renovation and addition to the Solomon R. Guggenheim Museum in New York.

Gwathmey's design features his architectural signature, pyramidal skylights, over a central gallery.

The 42,000-square-foot museum includes a cafe, gift shop, reception hall and sculpture garden.

Permanent collection:

Among the artists represented in the museum's collection are:

♦ Romare Beardon, born near Charlotte, who used rural North Carolina settings in much of his work.

♦ Minnie Evans, an "outsider artist" born near Wilmington, who gained fame for her mystical drawings and paintings despite having had no formal art training.

♦ Claude Howell, a Wilmington native who helped found the museum. His work focuses on the people and scenes of coastal North Carolina, and this region's distinctive light and color.

♦ Elisabeth Chant, an eccentric painter who taught many Wilmington artists including Claude Howell.

♦ Maude Gatewood, a contemporary Southern painter.

♦ Elliott Daingerfield, a leading Southern painter of the 19th Century.

The museum also has an important collection of North Carolina's famous Jugtown Pottery, and prints by Mary Cassatt, the American painter associated with the French Impressionists.

The museum grounds preserve Confederate earthworks from the Civil War. A paved walkway leads to the site of the 1865 Forks Road battle.

To get there: The museum is at South 17th Street and Independence Boulevard, south of Shipyard Boulevard. From the north, go through the intersection on southbound 17th and make a U-turn to the entrance.

Hours: 10 a.m.-5 p.m. Tuesday-Thursday and Saturday; 10 a.m.-8 p.m. Friday; 10:30 a.m.-4 p.m. Sunday. Adults $5, children 5-18 $2, under 5 free; family $8. 395-5999.

Several examples of the local scenes painted by the late Claude Howell.

A gallery of visionary works by self-taught artist Minnie Evans.

The fine arts
Galleries and groups

Wilmington seems to be a magnet for the arts, a favored place both for artists and craftsmen and for their patrons.

A few examples prove the point:

Wilmington-born painter Claude Howell spent his long creative life capturing the light of the Cape Fear Coast.

Every year, an international artists' colony gathers on Bald Head Island.

Cooperatives of artists have bought neglected old downtown buildings and created studios and performance spaces.

Retirees, school children and people of every age in between take classes and conduct music, dance and theater rehearsals in Wilmington's Community Arts Center, a former World War II USO building.

From Hampstead to Southport, with a dense concentration in historic downtown Wilmington, the region is full of galleries offering works both local and nationally known artists of every type.

And a host of groups exist for every imaginable artistic interest.

CAMERON ART MUSEUM
"The Letter" is part of the Cameron Art Museum's collection of prints by the American Impressionist painter Mary Cassatt.

Gallery Guide
A directory of *Wilmington Today*'s art advertisers, including samples of the works they represent.

American Pie
113 Dock St. 251-2131

In the heart of historic Downtown, American Pie is a delightful gallery of beautiful and unusual art by American artists. Offering a selection of handblown functional glass, jewelry, ceramics, art books, lamps and furniture and featuring the whistle art *See next page*

'Storyteller Chair'

********** American Pie **********
Folk Art & Contemporary Crafts

113 Dock Street
Wilmington • NC 28401
(910) 251-2131

in Historic
Downtown Wilmington

www.wilmingtontoday.com
51

McCLURE GALLERY
CUSTOM FRAMING & FINE ARTS

AN EXCLUSIVE COLLECTION OF IVEY HAYES
Limited Edition Giclee Prints • New Originals & All Time Favorites

FINE ART GICLEE PRINTS
On Canvas or Watercolor Paper

DISTINCTIVE CUSTOM FRAMING
Design Alternatives & Personal Service

ARCHIVAL GICLEE PRINTING SERVICE
Available for Artists & Photographers

Bradley Square • 5629 Oleander Drive • **794-9121**

Stimulate Your Imagination

Since 1985, New Elements Gallery has offered the best in fine art, glass, ceramics, jewelry and original home furnishings.

New Elements GALLERY

Discover the best Fine Art & Contemporary Craft

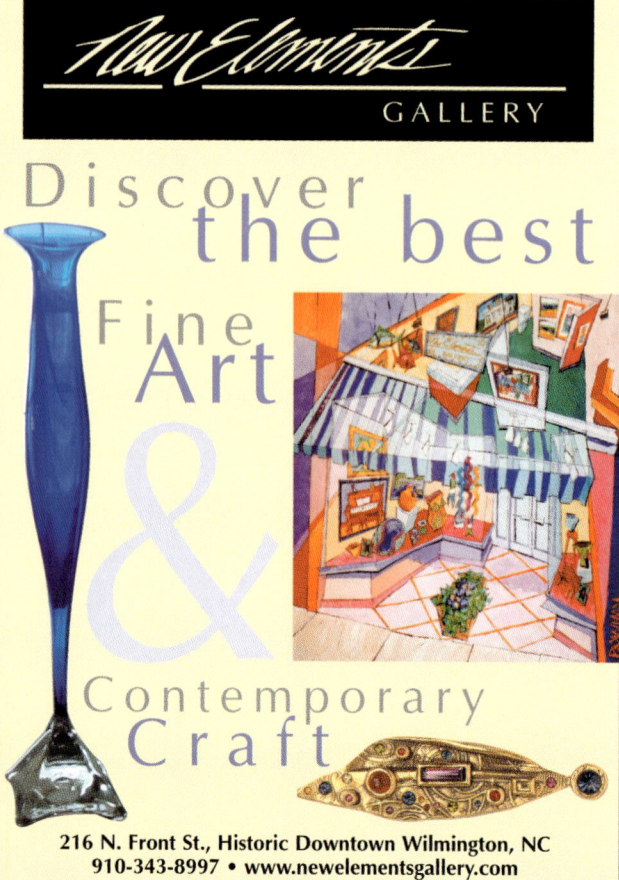

216 N. Front St., Historic Downtown Wilmington, NC
910-343-8997 • www.newelementsgallery.com

Continued from previous page
of Connie Roberts and the exciting art furniture and mirrors by Sticks. The gallery also features art by folk or outsider artists whose work has been seen in major museum shows.

McClure Gallery
5629 Oleander Drive #114   794-9121

'Club Scene, New York' by Ivey Hayes

Fine art photographer & master printer Joshua McClure has been reproducing art for over 25 years. He and designer/framer Mary Anne Sauer have formed a working gallery offering the finest art and design alternatives. It features fine art originals and archival giclee prints of stunning vibrancy and realism. A giclee is a high-quality reproduction, on fine quality paper or canvas, that matches the color fidelity of the original. Also offering custom framing and original work by local and national artists, featuring North Carolina artist Ivey Hayes.

New Elements Gallery
216 N. Front St. 343-8997

'Bald Head Dunes' by Jody Wrenn Rippy

Recognized as the area's leading art and craft gallery, New Elements offers a wide variety of work by regional and nationally known artists. In historic Downtown Wilmington since 1985, New Elements Gallery features original paintings and prints, sculpture, contemporary craft, jewelry and custom framing. Changing exhibitions are presented throughout the year. Visitors worldwide make a point of returning to enjoy this distinctive collection of fine art and craft.

www.wilmingtontoday.com

Continued from previous page

Simmons-Wright Gallery
1502 Market St. 762-1364

'Trio' by Leon Schenker

This gallery occupies a newly refurbished century-old building on Wilmington's Market Street. The unique and open space has been conceived as a destination and venue for anyone from the serious collector to the casual visitor. Sculptural walls and a rich color scheme accentuate the art, to capture all of the senses and resonate with an energy for all ages and levels of familiarity with art. Relax with a fine vintage in the balcony sofa bar overlooking the gallery.

ARTS GROUPS

This is a partial listing of local arts and crafts organizations.

Associated Artists of Southport: Exhibit spaces and studios at Franklin Square Gallery; regularly scheduled classes and juried exhibitions. 278-7560, 457-5450.

Cape Fear Camera Club: Sponsors competitions and annual exhibition. 799-2024.

Cape Fear Woodcarvers: 686-9518 ext. 29.

Columbus County Arts Council: Whiteville (910) 640-2787.

Community Arts Center: City-owned building at Second and Orange streets that provides space for art classes, rehearsals and performances. Includes Hannah Block Second Street Stage. 341-7860.

Historic Saint Thomas Preservation Society: Restores and operates 1845 church building at 208 Dock St. for community use. 763-4054.

No boundaries: Hosts international art colony on Bald Head Island every November. 392-4408.

Pender County Arts Council: Burgaw 259-4891.

WHQR: Public radio station sponsors exhibits in studio gallery, 254 North Front Street. 343-1640 WHQR web site.

Wilmington Art Association: Members exhibit at Wilmington Gallery in Chandler's Wharf, Water and Ann streets. Annual juried exhibition. 791-9471.

Wilmington Calligraphy Guild: Fine hand lettering. 392-5115.

CONVENTION & VISITORS BUREAU

Traditional crafts such as Polish 'Pisanki' Easter eggs flourish in greater Wilmington region.

SimmonsWright
GALLERY

Voted #1 art gallery by Encore Magazine's annual readers poll

largest selection of local and se regional art in the area
· wine tasting every tuesday

enjoy fine wines in our sofa lounge over looking our modern gallery space

Wilmington's *only* wine and fine art gallery

1502 Market Street Wilmington NC 28401 · 910.762.1364

www.wilmingtontoday.com

Performing arts
Theater, music and dance

THEATERS

City Stage: Restored intimate theater on the fifth floor of the 1898 Masonic Temple building. Hosts independent theater, comedy, cabaret and music. 21 N Front St. 342-0272.

Greenfield Lake Amphitheater. Off West Lake Shore Drive in Greenfield Park. Used for Shakespeare every June. Park office: 302 Willard St. 341-4604.

Hannah Block Second Street Stage. Community Arts Center is former USO building. Used by amateur and children's theater. 120 S. Second Street. 341-7860.

Kenan Auditorium: On UNC-Wilmington campus, used by University Theatre and others. Concerts by University Department of Music, Wilmington Symphony Orchestra, Wilmington Concert Association, visiting concerts by North Carolina Symphony. 601 South College Rd. 962-3500 or (800) 732-3643.

Scottish Rite Temple. Auditorium of Masonic temple. 1415 S. 17th St. 762-6452.

Thalian Hall Main Stage: A showplace since 1858. Restored in 1975. Seats 682 on three levels. 1990 addition added lobby, box office, rehearsal and storage spaces. 310 Chestnut St. behind City Hall. 343-3661 or (800) 523-2820.

Thalian Hall Studio Theatre: In Thalian Hall's 1990 wing, space with variable seating used for small theatrical productions. 343-3661 or (800) 523-2820.

THEATER COMPANIES:

Big Dawg Productions. Experimental productions; shows presented at Thalian & City Stage. 799-9321.

Cape Fear Community College Theatre Arts Education. Students. 762-2811

Cape Fear Shakespeare. Summer plays at Greenfield Amphitheater. 762-5303

Opera House Theatre Company. Produces major plays and experimental works in Thalian Hall theaters. 762-5234.

Pied Piper Theatre. Annual musical for schoolchildren sponsored by Junior League. 799-7405.

Rocking Chair Players. Based at county Senior Center. 799-4464

Stageworks Repertory Company. Family and adult audiences. 763-2563.

Thalian Association: Descended from a group founded in 1788. Plays in Thalian Hall and Second Street Stage. 251-1788.

Thalian Association Children's Theatre. Young casts. 251-1788.

University Theatre. UNCW students and staff at Kenan Auditorium. 962-3440.

Willis Richardson Players. Dramas by minority writers. 763-1889.

Thalian Hall, seen from the theater's upper balcony, was completed in 1858.

SCHEDULES
For current performance schedules and ticket information, and more detail about arts groups, see www.WilmingtonToday.com

N.C. Symphony plays at UNCW.

MUSIC & DANCE

Blues Society of the Lower Cape Fear: produces annual festival. 350-8822

Dance Theatre of Wilmington: Produces annual *Nutcracker*. 799-4704

Girls Choir of Wilmington: 799-5073.

North Carolina Jazz Festival: February shows at Hilton hotel. 763-8585.

North Carolina Symphony: Plays at Kenan Auditorium; box office 962-3500

Thalian Hall Main Attractions Series: Music & arts subscription series. 343-3664.

UNCW Jazz Ensembles: 962-3390

Girls Choir of Wilmington: 000-0000

Wilmington Boys Choir: 762-9693 ext. 212.

Chamber Music Society of Wilmington: sponsors touring chamber music acts. 763-1943.

Wilmington Choral Society: 458-5164.

Wilmington Concert Association: Subscription series brings touring classical artists to Kenan Auditorium. 962-3500.

Wilmington Symphony Orchestra: Performs at Kenan Auditorium. 791-9262.

A University Theater production on stage at UNCW's Kenan Auditorium

Nightlife
Clubs, comedy and dancing

Just as the beaches and historic attractions lure daytime visitors, Wilmington's restaurants, bars and nightclubs draw the nighttime crowd.

Downtown is the focal point for night life, with a broad spectrum of clubs offering music of all types and catering to audiences of all ages. Popular clubs are also found in other parts of town and at the beaches.

Wilmington is a "late" town. While some restaurants and bars have live music during cocktail or dinner hours, it's more typical for bands and other performers to start at 10 p.m. or later and play into the wee hours.

This has caused conflicts between Downtown's entertainment scene and another crowd that's helped make the neighborhood vibrant: its residents. With renovated apartments over many commercial spaces and new riverfront condos, the needs of residents who crave peace and quiet have to be balanced against the value of live entertainment for a healthy community.

A city noise ordinance, and other measures to limit the volume and hours at which live music is played are aimed to help keep harmony between these two vital constituencies.

The Downtown Area Revitalization Effort, a public-private economic development partnership, is working to keep Downtown's night life and residential life in balance.

JOHN MEYER
'Red Hat Club' ladies on North Front Street, out for a night on the town.

Schedules

For current performance schedules and ticket information, and more detail about music, entertainment and the arts, see our web site: **www.WilmingtonToday.com**

The Beat

This free music magazine provides current nightclub listings for WilmingtonToday.com

Other sources of current entertainment schedules include:

Encore, a free entertainment paper, published Thursdays.

Currents, the entertainment section of the Wilmington *Morning Star*. 50 cents, in Friday's paper.

Wilmington's new name in NightClub entertainment
- 15,000 square feet under one roof
- All Intelligent Lighting
- Full menu
- Laser light show
- VIP lounge
- Music, comedy, pool, video games

START EARLY, STAY LATE

fusion

Where the music and the vibe come together

Live radio broadcasts

**28 SOUTH FRONT STREET
DOWNTOWN WILMINGTON**
www.clubfusion.com

www.wilmingtontoday.com

56   www.wilmingtontoday.com

Shopping
Malls, stores and such

Whether your taste is a mall with everything under one roof, or the kinds of shops you find tucked away down a brick side street, our retail community is likely to find something to please you.

Here we offer some resources to help make your shopping easy, whether you're looking for something, or just browsing.

Key to advertisers
1. Airlie Gardens (page 63)
2. Alabama Theatre (page 61)
3. Alleigh's (page 35)
4. American Pie (page 51)
5. Birkenstock Comfortable Soles (page 58)
6. Blowing in the Wind (page 13)
7. Boca Bay (page 62)
8. Cafe Atlantique (page 63)
9. Cafe de France (page 36)
10. The Cape (pages 38 & 42)
11. Cape Fear Museum (page 17)
12. Cape Fear Serpentarium (page 49)
13. Circa 1922 (page 62)
14. Club Fusion (page 55)
15. Elijah's (page 38)
16. The Fish Market (page 34)
17. Fortune Hunter Charters (page 47)
18. Grouper Nancy's (page 37)
19. Heck of a Peck (page 34)
20. Henrietta III (page 26)
21. The Ivy Cottage (page 57)
22. Kayak Carolina & Carolina Coastal Adventures (page 27)
23. Ki Spa (page 13)
24. Lumina Station (page 2)
25. Magnolia Greens (page 43)
26. McClure Gallery (page 52)
27. New Elements Gallery (page 52)
28. Olympia (page 37)
29. The Pilot House (page 38)
20. Pottery Plus (page 59)
31. Reeds Jewelers (page 3)
32. Silver Jewelry Factory (page 59)
33. Simmons-Wright Gallery (page 53)
34. Sticky Fingers (page 36)
35. Studio Five (page 58)
36. Sundown Charters (page 46)
37. Tex's Tackle Shop (page 46)
38. Tomatoz (page 32)
39. Wilmington Trolley (28)
40. Wrightsville Beach Scenic Cruises (page 27)

Shopping Guide
A directory of advertisers.

Birkenstock Comfortable Soles
344 S. College Road. 790-3878

For comfort and style, check out our collection of shoes, sandals, clogs, socks and accesories for the whole family. We feature Birkenstocks and other comfort brands. Open 7 days. Shipping available. Toll-free (877) 902-3338.

Blowing in the Wind
312 Nutt St. 815-0907

Kites, kite boards, wind socks, flags, wind chimes: if the wind can make it move, we have it for you! On the parking lot level of The Cotton Exchange. Fly a kite on the beach, or learn how to fly with kiteboarding lessons.

Downtown Wilmington

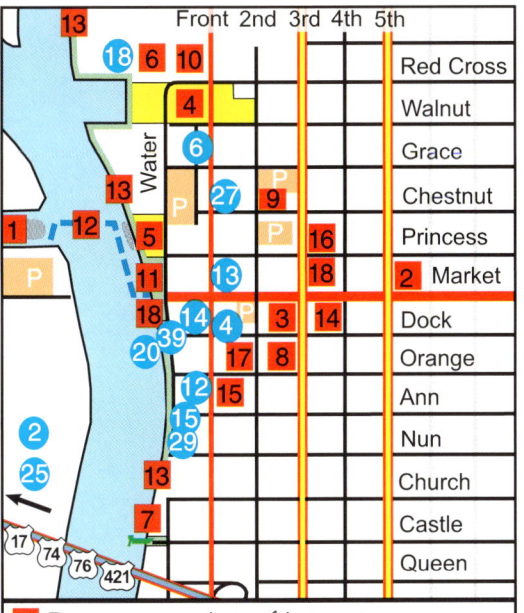

Downtown points of interest
1. Battleship North Carolina
2. Bellamy Mansion
3. Burgwin-Wright House
4. Cape Fear Community College
5. Coast Guard Dock & Cutter 'Diligence'
6. Coast Line Center
7. Dram Tree Park
8. Latimer House
9. Library
10. Railroad Museum
11. Riverfront Park
12. River Taxi
13. Riverwalk
14. St. James Churchyard
15. Smith-Anderson House
16. Thalian Hall/City Hall
17. USO/Arts Center
18. Visitor Centers
P. Public Parking

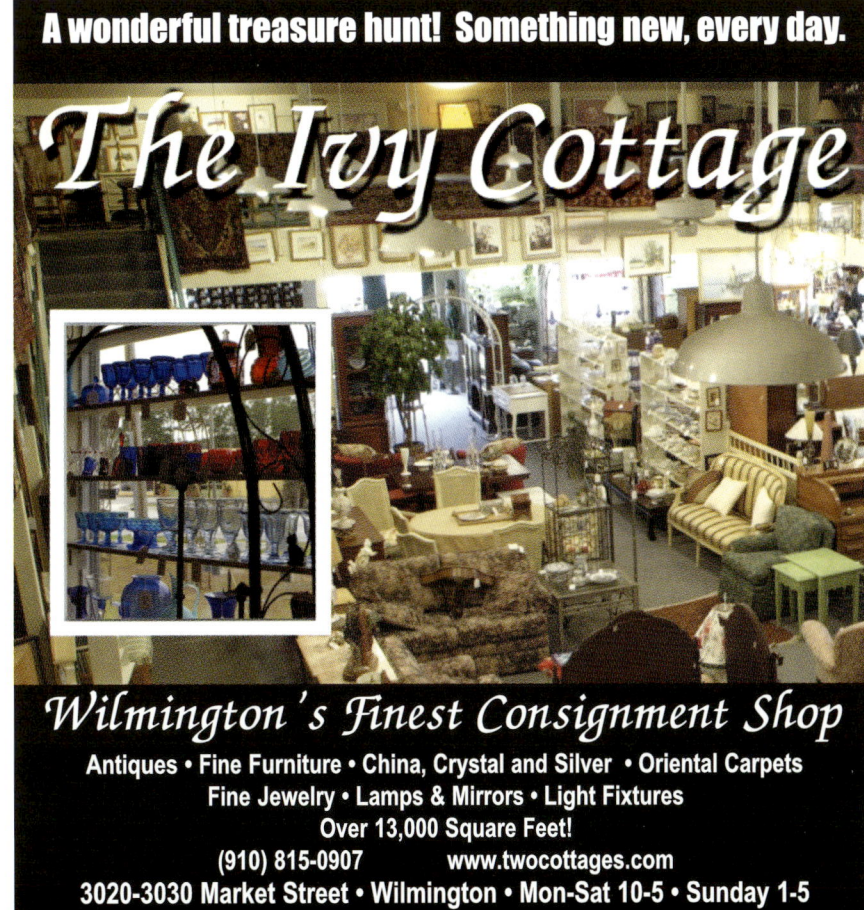

A wonderful treasure hunt! Something new, every day.
The Ivy Cottage
Wilmington's Finest Consignment Shop

Antiques • Fine Furniture • China, Crystal and Silver • Oriental Carpets
Fine Jewelry • Lamps & Mirrors • Light Fixtures
Over 13,000 Square Feet!

(910) 815-0907   www.twocottages.com
3020-3030 Market Street • Wilmington • Mon-Sat 10-5 • Sunday 1-5

www.wilmingtontoday.com

Presented by VINTAGE STUDIOS

Atlanta • High Point • Dallas • Los Angeles

STUDIO 5
At The Forum
910.509.9525

- Cool Furniture
- Architectural Iron
- Select Finds
- Arts & Antiques

vintagestudios.com

LiveOutsideTheBox.net

BIRKENSTOCK
Comfortable Soles

University Centre
344 South College Rd
(near Old Navy)
Wilmington
(910) 790-3878

Cameron Village
Raleigh, NC
(919) 828-9567

Eastgate Shopping Center
Chapel Hill, NC
(919) 933-1300

Broadway At The Beach
Myrtle Beach, SC
(843) 444-5663

SPECIALTY STORE BIRKENSTOCK

Open 7 Days A Week
Toll-Free 1-877-902-3338

The Ivy Cottage
3020 & 3030 Market St. 815-0907

Something for everyone in Wilmington's premier consignment shop. 13,000 square feet crammed with antiques, furniture, carpets, china, crystal, silver, artwork & chandeliers at great prices. Open 7 days. A wonderful treasure hunt!

Lumina Station
1900 Eastwood Road. 256-0900

Attractive low-country design incorporated into a beautiful tract with century-old hardwood trees. The mix of shops and restaurants offers fine apparel, gifts, art, jewelry, books, food and drink. Just before Wrightsville Beach drawbridge.

Pottery Plus
5744 Market St. 791-7522

Unlike any store on earth. Two acres of exciting decorative items for home and garden. Candles, silk and dried flowers, framed art, home & bath decor, accent furniture, outdoor furniture, fountains & statues, wicker, glassware -- and, of course, pottery!

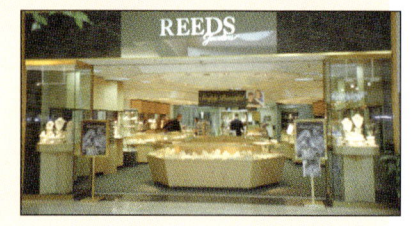

Reeds Jewelers
Westfield Independence. 799-6810

From the most basic to the most exquisite, Wilmington's premier jeweler offers a wide selection of fine diamonds, gold and gemstone jewelry. You'll find a superb collection of brand-name timepieces, including Rolex, plus elegant crystal and giftware. Open 7 days.

Silver Jewelry Factory
814 S. College Road. 392-3625

The area's biggest selection of silver jewelry, at great prices. Come see our exclusive collection of handcrafted Tommy J. nautical jewelry, 14k or silver; bracelets for men and women; shipwreck coins. By the way, please say hello to "Rocky" while you're here. Next to Dick's Sporting Goods.

throughout the U.S. Open 7 days, at The Forum. On line at liveoutsidethebox.net

Tex's Tackle
215 Old Eastwood Road. 791-1763

Southeastern North Carolina's largest, most complete tackle store. Salt and freshwater tackle, frozen bait, ice, drinks, line winding service and a knowledgeable staff. Conveniently located near the end of I-40 on your way to Wrightsville Beach. Call for the latest fishing report or to help you plan your next trip.

SHOPPING GUIDE ONLINE
For more information, including shopping center locations and web and email links to our advertisers, see **www.wilmingtontoday.com**

Studio 5
1119 Military Cutoff Road. 509-9525

Your secret source for select furniture, architectural antiques, decorative artifacts and accessories. Featuring work by American artisans, unveiling new "finds" weekly. Shipping available

---

Silver Jewelry Factory

Don't leave Wilmington without seeing the largest selection of Silver Jewelry in this coastal area at factory prices! If we don't have what you're looking for, no one does!

S. College Road, Wilmington, NC
University Square Shopping Center
(next to Dick's Sporting Goods)
(910) 392-3625

The Ultimate Shopping Adventure

EVERYDAY PRICES IN TOWN!

2 acres of...
- Home Decor • Floral
- Dinnerware/Glassware
- Decorative Garden
- Frames • Nautical Decor
- Wicker Furniture • Candles
- Baskets & Vases • Rugs
- Lamps & Shades
- Mirrors • Framed Art
- Accent Furniture

and... **Much MORE!**

Unlike any store on earth!

potteryplus®
910-791-7522

5744 Market Street MON-SAT 9am to 8pm • SUN 12am to 6pm
(Just 1/2 Mile North of the I-40 Overpass!)

www.wilmingtontoday.com

Day trips
Bright lights, country drives

Myrtle Beach

Just an hour's drive away, Myrtle Beach, S.C. is a world apart from Wilmington and the Cape Fear Coast.

It's famous for its beaches and for golf. But there are great beaches and great golf courses on this side of the state line, so our focus is on what sets Myrtle Beach apart.

It isn't the swimsuit-and-souvenir shops, which you'll find in any beach town. Lavish shows in large theaters or arenas and elaborate nature attractions draw day-trippers from the Wilmington area. These destinations are mostly grouped in a handful of large complexes. They include:

♦ Barefoot Landing, on U.S. 17 in North Myrtle Beach. Barefoot Landing features the Alabama Theatre, a stage for famous country music acts; the House of Blues, hosting well-known rock, r&b and jazz performers; and Alligator Adventure, a wildlife park.

♦ The Carolina Opry and Dixie Stampede, at the U.S. 17 Business-Bypass split. Their shows feature country music, comedy and horsemanship.

♦ Broadway at the Beach is a vast entertainment center with shopping areas, theme restaurants, miniature golf, hotels and the signature attractions: Ripley's Aquarium, Imax Theatre, and the Palace Theatre. The Palace features an Irish-dance show. Right across the bypass is NASCAR Speed Park and its cart track.

♦ Fantasy Harbour, on U.S. 501 across the Intracoastal Waterway, has jousting-knights dinner theater at Medieval Times, and celebrity impersonators at the Fantasy Theatre.

♦ Little River, just across the state line, is homeport for several casino boats that make day cruises offshore.

And, of course, there is the old Myrtle Beach. Along Ocean Boulevard you'll still find the taffy shops, arcades, ferris wheels and roller coasters that have drawn generations of families.

To get there: U.S. 17 south to North Myrtle Beach; U.S. 17 Bypass to Broadway; U.S. Business downtown.

AIRBORNE & SPECIAL OPERATIONS MUSEUM
C-47 transport dropped paratroopers behind German lines on D-Day.

Airborne & Special Operations Museum

Less than two hours away is Fort Bragg, home of the 82nd Airborne Division, part of the Army's first-line striking forces. This new museum tells the story of Army airborne operations from World War II to the present.

Exhibits include a Douglas C-47 "Skytrain," the plane that dropped paratroopers on the D-Day battlefields of Normandy. The museum has a rare Waco CG-4A glider, a type also used in the D-Day invasion.

Helicopters and light tanks represent Vietnam and more recent wars.

The museum has a "Vistascope" theater and a simulator that gives a feel for the airborne experience.

Hours: 10 a.m. to 5 p.m. Tues- Sat. (910) 483-3003. Free admission. Theater and motion simulator $3 each; $5 for both. Children under 8 free with paying adult.

To get there: U.S. 74-76 west 17 miles to Riegelwood exit. Right (north) on N.C. 87 to Fayetteville. Exit 104B, Hay Street, right to Bragg Boulevard. The museum is at 100 Bragg Blvd.

At Fort Bragg are two more specialized military museums:

82nd Airborne Division Museum: Ardennes & Gela streets. 432-5307.

JFK Special Warfare Museum: On the "Green Berets" and special ops. Ardennes & Marion streets. 432-4272.

Rural scenes

DUPLIN TOURISM

Off Interstate 40

Rose Hill is home to Duplin Winery. Its vineyards are mostly planted in native Scuppernong and Muscadine grapes. Tasting tours, vineyard tours and dinner shows makes the winery a favorite attraction.

Rose Hill's other claim to fame is the World Largest Frying Pan. It's on display in the town park.

To get there: From I-40, Exit 380.

Nearby in Kenansville are Liberty Hall, a museum of pre-Civil War life (296-2175) and the Cowan Museum (296-2149.) For more, see page 19.

North Carolina 87

The shortest way to Fayetteville, N.C. 87 is also the prettiest road in the region. It's a little-traveled route that offers unspoiled vistas of woods and streams, working farms, historic churches, and some intriguing side trips.

Some sights to look for along 87:

♦ Locks and dams. Seldom used by barges these days, they are popular fishing and picnicking spots.

♦ The Elwell Ferry. Last of the cable ferries that once crossed rivers throughout the Coastal Plain, this little craft shuttles back and forth, carrying two cars at a time, across a remote stretch of the Cape Fear River.

www.wilmingtontoday.com

ONE THE SHOW

6 NIGHTS A WEEK THRU OCTOBER 24TH!

10 Years of Entertaining America!

3/8	OAK RIDGE BOYS
3/15	DRIFTERS, COASTERS & PLATTERS
4/5	THE GATLIN BROTHERS
4/12	RAY PRICE
4/13	EDDIE MILES Salute To Elvis
4/19	MEL TILLIS
5/2, 3	GEORGE JONES
5/11	EDDIE MILES Salute To Elvis
6/8	EDDIE MILES Salute To Elvis
6/20	DRIFTERS, COASTERS & PLATTERS
6/26	CHARLIE DANIELS
7/24	BILLY RAY CYRUS
8/1	TANYA TUCKER
8/8	LORETTA LYNN
8/16	DIAMOND RIO
8/22	TEMPTATIONS & SUPREMES
8/24	EDDIE MILES Salute To Elvis
8/30	RICKY VAN SHELTON
9/6	GLENN MILLER ORCHESTRA
9/13	CRYSTAL GAYLE
9/20	CHARLEY PRIDE
9/27	LORRIE MORGAN
9/28	EDDIE MILES Salute To Elvis
10/4	THE LETTERMEN
10/11	PORTER WAGONER W/ LITTLE JIMMY DICKENS
10/18	DRIFTERS, COASTERS & PLATTERS
10/25	OAK RIDGE BOYS
11/1	CHRISTMAS SHOW Premieres thru Dec. 31
11/9	EDDIE MILES Salute To Elvis
11/16	CAMMY AWARDS 3PM

ALL SHOWS AT 7PM UNLESS NOTED.
SHOWS ADDED WEEKLY SO CALL OR LOG ON FOR LATEST!

FAMILY NIGHTS!
KIDS FREE JUNE - AUGUST!
Mondays, Wednesdays & Saturdays
(2 kids per paid adult)

ALABAMA THEATRE
BAREFOOT LANDING

Reservations -
843-272-1111
800-342-2262

www.alabama-theatre.com

boca bay
tapas style

You are cordially invited to join us at the wine bar, inside or fountain side to enjoy small plate cuisine at its finest, featuring sushi, fresh seafood, pasta, thai delicacies and colossal confections.

2025 Eastwood Rd.
256-1887

Circa 1922

- Tapas style menu
- Charming 1920's decor
- Extensive array of wines

8 North Front Street
Downtown Wilmington
762.1022